Table of Contents

I. Diagnosis — 3
    A. Mission — 3
    B. Objectives — 3
    C. Corporate Strategy — 3
    D. Policies — 3
        1. Diversity — 3
        2. Ethical Standards/Code of Conduct — 4
        3. Suppliers — 4
        4. HR — 4
    E. Strategic Managers and Board — 5
        1. Senior Level Executives — 6
        2. Corporate Governance — 15
        3. Responsibilities — 16
        4. Board Committees — 19
        5. Director Compensation — 19
    F. Generic Industry Type — 20
        1. IBIS World Report 44814 — 21
    G. Organization Structure — 29
    H. Financial Analysis — 31
        1. Key Financial Ratios – Gap — 31
        2. Key Financial Ratios – TJ Maxx — 32
        3. Key Financial Ratios – Ross — 33
        4. Key Financial Ratios – American Eagle — 34
        5. Revenue — 35
        6. Net Income — 36
        7. Gross Profit Margin — 37
        8. Operating Profit Margin — 38
        9. Return on Total Asset — 39
        10. Return on Stockholder's Equity — 40
        11. Current Ratio — 41
        12. Debt to Asset Ratio — 42
        13. Inventory Turnover Ratio — 43
        14. COGS / Sales % — 44
        15. SG&A / Sales — 45
        16. Altman's — 46

17. Tobin's Q	47
18. DuPont Analysis	48
19. Stock Analysis	49
19. SWOT Analysis	50
Internal – Strengths, Weaknesses	50
External – Opportunities, Threats	52
J. Market Share Data Graph	57
II. Focal Points for Action	**60**
1. Risk Factors	60
2. Short Range	61
3. Long Range	61
III. Alternatives	**61**
IV. Decision and Recommendations	**66**
V. Implementation	**68**
VI. Bibliography	**70**

Diagnosis
Mission
"Gap, Inc. is a brand-builder. We create emotional connections with customers around the world through inspiring product design, unique store experiences, and compelling marketing."

Purpose - "Our purpose? Simply, to make it easier for you to express your personal style throughout your life. We have more than 150,000 passionate, talented people around the world who help bring this purpose to life for our customers."

Objectives
The GAP's objectives are to ensure that all employees and the company's Board of Directors (directors) not only meet legal requirements around the world, but also operate responsibly and with integrity in everything they do. (www.gapinc.com)

Corporate Strategy
The GAP's corporate strategy is based on diversity; The GAP meets all economic classes with their apparel. Old Navy's value priced clothing and accessories enable The Gap to progress during economic down turns. The Banana Republic's trendy products present consumers with more fashion assortment during economic growth. International expansion is another corporate strategy for this retailer; The GAP is continuously aimed at bridging the business-casual attire "gap". Outsourcing has become a significant factor in the success of The GAP, Inc. The textile industry has been an essential driving force in China's economy for many years. Outsourcing production to China has become a widespread norm for international business firms in this present time. E-commerce growth is a strategy The GAP, Inc. continuously works to improve. The GAP's website is aimed at increasing user-friendliness, speed and security. The GAP services 90 countries with their 5 consumer brands. GAP's number one corporate strategy is pleasing customers. The GAP, Inc. is invested in hearing the wants/needs of their customers. The GAP, Inc. knew in hard economic times value maximization was on the forefront of their consumers' minds, and now offers Gap Outlet and Banana Republic Factory Stores to meet the demand for value seekers. The GAP, Inc. has recognized the importance of the woman's role in shopping for the whole family, and focuses their marketing tactics on women with families in hope of increasing market share.

Policies

Diversity
As a global company, we know that appreciating and understanding the
diversity of our customers, employees and partners around the world helps make us successful. We value the diversity of thought, experience and perspectives of our customers. Embracing diversity stimulates innovation in our products and helps us improve our store experience. That enables us to create an inviting and inclusive place to work and to shop. We maintain our commitment to diversity with workplace policies that ensure we do what's right, and treat our

customers and each other with integrity and respect. (www.gapinc.com).

Ethical Standards/Code of Conduct
"is a commitment we make to our shareholders, customers and each other not only out of a legal obligation, but because it's the right thing to do. Our success is built on trust, along with a reputation for transparency and quality in everything we do. We each make important contributions to protecting our company and its reputation. Recognizing right from wrong, and understanding the ethical implications of our choices, is fundamental to doing what's right at Gap Inc. We are each responsible for applying the standards outlined in our Code of Business Conduct to our work, every day."
(http://www.gapinc.com/content/dam/gapincsite/documents/COBC/COBC_english.pdf)

Suppliers
To hold suppliers accountable for a safe, healthy, and humane workplace, Gap Inc. has traveled over the past decade from what was primarily a policing model based on a corps of internal monitors to a more collaborative partnership in which factory owners and managers are expected to take more responsibility, or "ownership," for conditions on their factory floors. This article attempts to share some key aspects of this journey toward ongoing social compliance, to demystify what a company should and can do, and to discuss in detail one resource—the Social Accountability 8000 (SA8000) workplace standard and its associated certification system that provides a way to empower factory management and help buyers manage the demands for socially responsible sourcing. Although the supply chains of clothing and shoe companies were the first to come under public scrutiny, the spotlight of stakeholder attention continues to expand. It is no longer a question of if a company with a global supply chain will be held accountable for workplace standards at factories it owns or with which it contracts, but rather when.

HR
"We have a long history of conducting our business in a responsible manner. Since the company's founding in 1969, we've worked to meet the aspiration of our co-founders Doris and Don Fisher to "do more than sell clothes." Our company's core values seek to ensure that the individuals who work at Gap Inc. and within our global supply chain are treated with fairness, dignity and respect.
Our team of Social Responsibility Specialists annually inspected nearly 100% of the factories we source with around the world; 50% of these inspections were unannounced, surprise inspections. But we recognize that monitoring alone is not enough to improve working conditions and create opportunity for garment workers. We also build partnerships and aim to share accountability among companies, vendors, workers and other key stakeholders.

We are seeking to further align our human rights practices with the United Nation's Guiding Principles on Business and Human Rights, and have asked Shift to comment on our supply chain practices in this report. Shift is a leading non-profit center that works with governments, businesses and stakeholders to put the UN Guiding Principles into practice. Gap Inc.'s focus on understanding the root causes of issues in our supply chain helps us better address the underlying causes of poor working conditions so that the solutions we support will truly last. Furthermore, our Code of Vendor Conduct explicitly outlines workers' rights to "lawfully and peacefully associate, organize or bargain collectively," enabling workers in Gap's supply chain to engage with management on fair wages, sufficient benefits, and fair and safe working conditions." (www.gapinc.com)

Strategic Managers and Board

Name	Job Title	Board	Compensation
Glenn K. Murphy	Chairman and Chief Executive Officer	Executive Board	24627812 USD
Bob L. Martin	Lead Independent Director	Non Executive Board	249980 USD
Adrian D. P. Bellamy	Director	Non Executive Board	223433 USD
Domenico De Sole	Director	Non Executive Board	213980 USD
Robert J. Fisher	Director	Non Executive Board	212980 USD
William S. Fisher	Director	Non Executive Board	194980 USD
Isabella D. Goren	Director	Non Executive Board	201577 USD
Jorge P. Montoya	Director	Non Executive Board	226980 USD
Mayo A. Shattuck III	Director	Non Executive Board	247980 USD
Katherine Tsang	Director	Non Executive Board	217480 USD
Padmasree Warrior	Director	Non Executive Board	
Sabrina Simmons	Executive Vice President and Chief Financial Officer	Senior Management	5686946 USD
Stephen Sunnucks	Global President, Gap	Senior Management	5824146 USD
Stefan Larsson	Global President, Old Navy	Senior Management	9697324 USD
Jack Calhoun	Global President, Banana Republic	Senior Management	
Arthur Peck	President, Growth, Innovation and Digital	Senior Management	4775058 USD
Michelle Banks	Executive Vice President, General Counsel, Corporate Secretary and Chief Compliance Officer	Senior Management	
Sonia Syngal	Executive Vice President, Global Supply Chain	Senior Management	
John T. Keiser	Executive Vice President and Chief Information Officer	Senior Management	
Eva Sage-Gavin	Executive Vice President, Global Human Resources and Corporate Affairs	Senior Management	
David Zoba	Senior Vice President, Global Real Estate	Senior Management	

Senior Level Executives

Glen K. Murphy, Chairman and Chief Executive Officer – Gap, Inc.

Glenn Murphy joined Gap Inc. as Chairman of the Board and Chief Executive Officer in July 2007. Under Glenn's leadership, the company has successfully driven bottom line earnings growth by focusing on healthy margins and expense management. The company's executive management team is focused on restoring the health of the brands and pursuing growth opportunities overseas through its online channels, franchise operations and international expansion.

Glenn has more than 20 years of retail experience and has successfully led diverse retail businesses and brands in the areas of food, health and beauty, and books. He has an established track record as a decisive, in-charge leader who has revitalized established retail brands.

From 2001 to 2007, Glenn served as Chairman and Chief Executive Officer of Shoppers Drug Mart, Canada's largest drug store chain, delivering 22 consecutive quarters of year-over-year revenue growth.

Prior to Shoppers Drug Mart, Glenn served as President and Chief Executive Officer of Chapters, Canada's leading book retailer. He also had a 14-year career with Loblaw Companies Ltd, Canada's largest food distributor and supermarket chain, and started his career at A.C. Nielsen, the world's leading marketing information company.

Glenn serves as the chairman of the Gap Foundation Board of Trustees. He holds a B.A. from the University of Western Ontario.

Sabrina Simmons, EVP and Chief Financial Officer – Gap, Inc.

Sabrina Simmons is Executive Vice President and Chief Financial Officer of Gap Inc. In this role, she oversees all global financial departments, including controllership, corporate financial planning and analysis, investor relations, treasury, tax, risk management, internal audit and the corporate shared service center, and also has accountability for brand finance along with the company's brand presidents.

Since joining Gap Inc. in 2001, Sabrina has progressed through positions of increasing responsibility from vice president and treasurer to executive vice president. Simmons was appointed CFO in January 2008.

During her tenure, she has been instrumental in instilling financial discipline throughout the organization and developing the capital structure framework that has delivered increasing shareholder distributions while maintaining a strong balance sheet.

Before coming to Gap, Sabrina was chief financial officer and an executive member of the Board of Directors of Sygen International PLC, a British genetics company. Prior to Sygen, Simmons spent five years at Levi Strauss & Co., where she was assistant treasurer. She also spent several years at Hewlett Packard Company and KPMG.

Sabrina received her B.S. in Finance from the University of California, Berkeley where she was also bestowed the award of Regent Scholar, and received her M.B.A. from the Anderson School at the University of California, Los Angeles. Sabrina serves as a member of the Gap Foundation Board of Trustees.

Steve Sunnucks, Global President – Gap, Inc.

Steve Sunnucks is the global president of Gap brand, with responsibility for managing all channels and markets for Gap brand around the world.

Most recently, Steve served as the president of Gap Inc.'s International division, where he was responsible for the business outside North America, which included about 750 stores across 40 countries, including eight of the world's top 10 apparel retail markets. Under his leadership, Gap Inc. expanded its international footprint in Europe with company-operated stores, including the launch of Banana Republic in Europe and introduction of Old Navy outside of North American for the first the time. The company also has reached new customers with franchise stores in Asia, Australia, Latin America, Eastern Europe, and Russia.

In his 30-year career in retail, Steve has established a strong track record in global apparel, holding senior leadership roles with large, well-known retailers including Marks & Spencer, Sainsbury and the Burton Group (now Arcadia).

Prior to joining Gap Inc. in 2005, he spent four years as chief executive officer of New Look, a large, publicly listed European clothing retailer with over 700 stores in the U.K., Ireland and France. During his term as CEO, Steve repositioned the company as a fast-fashion brand, launched and rolled out a new large store format and introduced new product categories

Steve graduated from Sheffield University in England with an honors degree in economics.

Michelle Banks, EVP, General Counselor, Corporate Secretary, Chief Compliance Officer – Gap, Inc.

Michelle Banks is Executive Vice President, General Counsel, Corporate Secretary and Chief Compliance Officer of Gap Inc.

In addition to the global legal function, Michelle oversees the Company's global equity administration; franchise services; privacy; and social and environmental responsibility functions. She joined Gap Inc. in 1999. Prior to becoming General Counsel in 2006, Michelle established and led the Company's corporate governance and corporate compliance functions within the legal department.

Before joining Gap Inc., Michelle was in-house legal counsel for the NBA's Golden State Warriors, and prior to that, worked in Japan as American counsel for ITOCHU Corporation. She was also associated with several law firms, including Morrison & Foerster in California and New York, focusing on corporate finance and international commercial transactions.

Michelle graduated from UCLA with degrees in Law and Economics, and was admitted to the California bar in 1988. She serves on the Executive Committees of the Board of Directors of Minority Corporate Counsel Association and United Way of the Bay Area. She is Chair of the General Counsel Forum of the National Retail Association and serves on the American Bar Association's Commission on Women in the Profession.

Sonia Syngal, EVP, Global Supply Chain – Gap, Inc.

Sonia Syngal is Executive Vice President of Global Supply Chain for Gap Inc. Sonia is responsible for managing Gap Inc.'s global supply chain, which includes the company's logistics network and sourcing operations for both apparel and non-apparel, spanning nearly 40 countries.

Sonia brings a broad range of brand and supply chain strategy experience to the role. Since joining Gap Inc. in 2004, she has served in key leadership roles including Vice President of Corporate Sourcing and then Global Production & Supply Chain. During this time, she was instrumental in delivering production and sourcing strategies for Gap, Banana Republic and Old Navy. Sonia also served in several general management roles including Senior Vice President for Gap Inc.'s International Outlet division and Managing Director for Gap Inc.'s Europe business. Most recently, she was Senior Vice President of Old Navy's International division where she led the successful expansion of the brand in Japan and set the strategies for Old Navy's global growth.

Prior to joining Gap Inc., Sonia had a long career in supply chain and manufacturing, including nearly 10 years at Sun Microsystems where she led manufacturing operations, logistics and supply chain management during a time of rapid growth.

Sonia holds a Master's degree in Manufacturing Systems Engineering from Stanford University, and a Bachelor's degree in Mechanical Engineering from Kettering University. She is a guest lecturer at the Stanford School of Business.

Tom Keiser, EVP, Global Product Operations – Gap, Inc.

Tom Keiser is Gap Inc. Executive Vice President of Global Product Operations. In this role, Tom is responsible for the design and execution of one of Gap Inc.'s key priorities, Seamless Inventory. The objective of Seamless Inventory is to significantly reduce stranded inventory and improve margin for each of our Global Brands.

Tom is a proven retail and IT executive with significant experience building global operating platforms. Through his 25-year career, Tom has led major global initiatives for consumer product and retail companies. Tom joined Gap Inc. in 2010 as the company's Chief Information Officer.

Prior to joining Gap Inc., Tom was EVP and CIO for Limited Brands (now L Brands), where he spearheaded a multi-year transformational program which built a new business and technology retail operating model. During 12 years with Ernst & Young, he gained significant international expertise, managing the rollout of major systems in Europe and the Middle East for a range of companies, including the Coca-Cola Company. Tom began his career at BellSouth as a programmer analyst.

Tom currently serves as a trustee for Gap Foundation, as the Chair of the Board for Big Brothers Big Sisters of the Bay Area, and is Chair of the Advisory Board for The Fisher CIO Leadership Program at the Haas School of Business at UC Berkeley. Tom received a bachelor's degree from the University of West Florida.

David Zoba, SVP, Global Real Estate – Gap, Inc.

David Zoba is Senior Vice President of Global Real Estate. In this role, he works closely with Gap Inc.'s brand presidents and International business leaders in developing and delivering on the company's strategies to optimize its global real estate fleet.

David began as a real estate attorney on Wall Street and quickly moved into shopping centers and corporate real estate. He joined The Limited in the mid-1990s to lead real estate law, and then expanded his responsibility significantly to other areas during his seven years with the company. He subsequently worked for Galyan's Trading Company, Inc., whereas EVP he helped create and launch a specialty sporting goods retailer that later became part of Dick's Sporting Goods. Most recently, David was principal and chief operating officer for Steiner + Associates, one of the country's most respected mixed-use retail developers.

David earned his undergraduate degree from Harvard University and attended the London School of Economics for graduate studies. David has a J.D. from Case Western Reserve University Law School.

Stefan Larsson, Global President – Old Navy

Stefan joined Gap Inc. after a highly successful career at Swedish retailer, Hennes & Mauritz (H&M), spanning nearly 15 years.

He most recently served as head of Global Sales with functional responsibility for about 2,300 stores and nearly all of the company's $17 billion in annual sales. This role, which reported to the CEO, encompassed all aspects of the business that are customer-facing: product merchandising, visual merchandising, store operations, store design and development, inventory management, and customer service.

Previously, Stefan was responsible for overseeing H&M's global expansion, with responsibility for real estate, store design and store construction. Earlier in his career at H&M, he lived in California and led the company's launch of H&M on the West Coast of the United States, and spent nearly seven years in numerous global roles with responsibility for product, including merchandising, assortment development, planning and production for the company.

Stefan earned a M.Sc. in Business Administration jointly from the Swedish School of Economics and Business Administration, in Finland, and Jonkoping International Business School, in Sweden.

Jack Calhoun, Global President – Banana Republic

Jack Calhoun is global president of Banana Republic. He is responsible for managing all channels and markets for Banana Republic around the world.

This position expands the role Jack had previously, serving as president of Banana Republic North America. In that role, he grew sales and positioned Banana Republic as the go-to brand for professionals seeking modern and versatile workplace style. Previously, as executive vice president of Merchandising and Marketing at Banana Republic, he oversaw all aspects of merchandising and marketing and was instrumental in developing the brand's growth strategies. He successfully led growth initiatives including launching an elevated handbag line, a personal care suite of fragrances, and an eyewear collection.

Jack joined Gap Inc. in 2003, coming from Charles Schwab & Co., where he was the executive vice president of Brand Management and Advertising. Prior to that, he spent six years leading teams at Foote, Cone & Belding and Young & Rubicam, where he served as general manager of the San Francisco office. He also held marketing positions at Levi Strauss & Company and The Procter & Gamble Company.

Jack received a B.S. from Purdue University an M.B.A. from Harvard Business School and attended Indiana University School of Music.

Jack currently serves on the Board of Directors of the San Francisco Opera, one of the world's leading opera companies. He also served for five years on the Board of Directors of the national not-for-profit GLAAD (Gay and Lesbian Alliance Against Defamation) as well as on the Board of Directors of the Mitchell Gold furniture company.

Corporate Governance

Role of the Board

The board is responsible for oversight of the business, affairs and integrity of the company, determination of the company's mission, long-term strategy and objectives, and oversight of the company's risks while evaluating and directing implementation of company controls and procedures.

The board may delegate some of its responsibilities to the committees of the board of directors.

Composition and Qualifications of the Board of Directors

(a) **Size of the Board.** As provided by the company's Bylaws and by resolution of the board of directors, the current number of board members can vary according to the board's needs. The number of directors is currently set at 10.

(b) **Mix of Management Directors and Independent Directors.** The board believes that as a matter of policy there should be at least a majority of independent directors as defined under SEC and NYSE rules ("Independent" directors) on the board. In addition, the board believes that it is most desirable for Independent directors to constitute two-thirds or more of the board, and is committed to maintaining such levels barring unforeseen circumstances, including mid-year resignations. For a nominee to be considered an Independent director, the board must also affirmatively determine that the director has no material relationship with Gap Inc. Directors who are officers or employees of the company are considered management directors ("Management" directors). The board may also consist of directors who are not officers or employees of the company but who are also not considered independent (these directors with the Independent directors are considered "Non-Management" directors).

(c) **Qualifications and Diversity of Board Members.** All board members possess certain core competencies, some of which may include experience in retail, consumer products, international business/markets, real estate, store operations, logistics, product design, merchandising, marketing, general operations, strategy, human resources, technology, media or public relations, finance or accounting, or experience as a CEO or CFO. In addition to having one or more of these core competencies, board member nominees are identified and considered on the basis of knowledge, experience, integrity, leadership, reputation, and ability to understand the company's business. The board believes that diversity, including differences in backgrounds, qualifications, experiences, and personal characteristics, including gender and ethnicity/race, is important to the effectiveness of the board's oversight of the company. Nominees are pre-screened to ensure each candidate has qualifications which complement the overall core competencies of the board. The screening process includes conducting a background evaluation and an independence determination.

(d) **Selection of New Board Members.** The Governance and Nominating Committee has the responsibility to identify, screen, and recommend qualified candidates to the board. Qualified candidates are interviewed by the Chairman and CEO as well as at least two Independent directors. Certain other directors and members of management will interview each candidate as requested by the Chairman, CEO or chair of the Governance and Nominating Committee. In addition, the committee will consider candidates recommended by shareholders in the manner set forth in the Bylaws.

(e) **Director Election Vote Response.** At any meeting of the shareholders at which a director is not elected in accordance with the Bylaws, that director shall submit to the Board an offer letter of resignation, subject to board acceptance. The Governance and Nominating Committee will consider the offer of resignation and will recommend to the board the action to be taken. The board shall act promptly with respect to each such letter of resignation and shall promptly notify the director concerned of its decision. The board's decision would be disclosed publicly within 90 days from the date of certification of the election results.

Board Members and Responsibilities

Adrian D. P. Bellamy
Director since 1995. Former chairman of The Body Shop International plc, personal care retailer. Chairman of Reckitt Benckiser plc. Chairman of Williams-Sonoma, Inc.
- Chairman of the Compensation and Management Development Committee
- Member of the Governance and Nominating Committee

Domenico De Sole
Director since 2004. Chairman of Tom Ford International, a luxury retailer. Former President and Chief Executive Officer of Gucci Group NV, a luxury multi-brand company. Director of Newell Rubbermaid, Inc.
- Member of the Compensation and Management Development Committee

Robert J. Fisher
Director since 1990. Managing Director Pisces, Inc. an investment group. Former Chairman, Interim CEO and executive of the company. (Robert J. Fisher is the son of Doris F. and Donald G. Fisher.)
- Member of the Governance and Nominating Committee

William S. Fisher
Director since 2009. Chief Executive Officer of Manzanita Capital Limited, a private equity fund. Former executive of the company. Founder of Manzanita Capital. (William S. Fisher is the son of Doris F. and Donald G. Fisher.)
- Does not sit on any board committees

Bella Goren
Director since 2011. Chief Financial Officer of AMR Corporation and American Airlines, Inc.
- Member of the Audit and Finance Committee

Bob L. Martin
Lead Independent Director. Director since 2002. Chief Executive Officer* of Mcon Management Services, Ltd., a consulting company; Operating Partner of The Stephens Group, LLC., a private equity group; former President and Chief Executive Officer of Wal-Mart International. Director of Conn's, Inc.
- Member of the Compensation and Management Development Committee
- Chairman of the Governance and Nominating Committee

* Mr. Martin's position with Mcon Management Services, Ltd. is a part-time commitment.

Jorge P. Montoya
Director since 2004. Former executive of The Procter & Gamble Company. Director of the Kroger Co.
- Member of the Audit and Finance Committee

Glenn K. Murphy
Director since 2007. Chairman and Chief Executive Officer.
- Does not sit on any board committees.

Mayo A. Shattuck III
Director since 2002. Executive Chairman of Exelon Corporation, an energy company. Director of Capital One Financial Corporation.
- Chairman of the Audit and Finance Committee
- Member of the Governance and Nominating Committee

Katherine Tsang
Director since 2010. Chairperson, Greater China Standard Chartered Bank PLC. Chairs the boards of Standard Chartered Bank (Hong Kong) Limited, Standard Chartered Bank (China) Limited and Standard Chartered Bank (Taiwan) Limited.

- Member of the Compensation and Management Development Committee

Padmasree Warrior

Director since 2013. Chief Technology Officer and Chief Strategy Officer of Cisco Systems. Former CTO of Motorola.

- Does not sit on any committees.

Board Committees

Director	Audit & Finance	Compensation & Mgmt Devel.	Gov'nce & Nominating
Independent			
Adrian D. P. Bellamy		C	M
Domenico De Sole		M	
Robert J. Fisher			M
William S. Fisher			
Bella Goren	M		
Bob L. Martin		M	C
Jorge P. Montoya	M		
Mayo A. Shattuck III	C		M
Katherine Tsang		M	
Padmasree Warrior			
Other			

Director Compensation

The Non-Management directors' annual base retainer is currently $75,000 per annum, plus an attendance fee of $2,000 for each regularly scheduled committee meeting attended. Non-management directors who primarily reside outside of North America receive a fee of $2,000 for attendance at each board and/or committee meeting requiring travel to the United States. The Governance and Nominating Committee Chair receives an additional retainer of $15,000 per annum. The Audit and Finance Committee Chair and the Compensation and Management Development Committee Chair each receive an additional retainer of $20,000 per annum. The

Lead Independent director receives an additional retainer of $25,000 per annum. In addition, Non-Management directors are eligible to receive stock unit awards according to a pre-determined formula as follows: (i) upon appointment each new Non-Management director is awarded units equal to $140,000 at the then-current fair market value; and (ii) annually, each continuing Non-Management director is awarded units equal to $140,000 at the then-current fair market value (recently appointed Non-Management directors first annual stock unit grant shall be prorated based on the number of days that the director has served between the appointment date and the first annual stock unit grant). Normally, the stock units are immediately vested as of the award date with payment in shares deferred for three years unless further deferred at the election of the Non-Management director.

Generic Industry Type
44814-Family Clothing Stores in the U.S.

The Family Clothing Stores in the US - 44814 is fragmented meaning there are no clear leaders in the industry. It is also a mature in its industry life cycle. The average growth rate for the next 5 years is 2.2%. Households account for 99.5% of the market, while the rest of the buyers include retailers, wholesalers and other commercial buyers. The breakdown is as follows:
- Commercial buyers 5%
- Children age 9 and under 7%
- Seniors age 65 and over 10%
- Generation Y 22.5%
- Baby boomers 24.5%
- Generation X 35.5%

Generation X has the most potential for growth in the Family Clothing Stores in US Industry. This segment includes individuals who purchase clothing for themselves and for their children as well as their significant others. This amount has expanded over the past five years. They are more price conscious than younger and older generations because the responsibility of having a family is most often experienced during this stage of life.

Family retailers stock a general line of new clothing for men, women and children, without specializing in apparel for an individual or age group. These establishments may also provide basic alterations, such as hemming, taking in or letting out seams and lengthening and shortening.

IBIS World Report 44814

Industry definition	**Family Clothing Stores - 44814** Family retailers stock a general line of new clothing for men, women and children, without specializing in apparel for an individual or age group. These establishments may also provide basic alterations, such as hemming, taking in or letting out seams and lengthening and shortening. 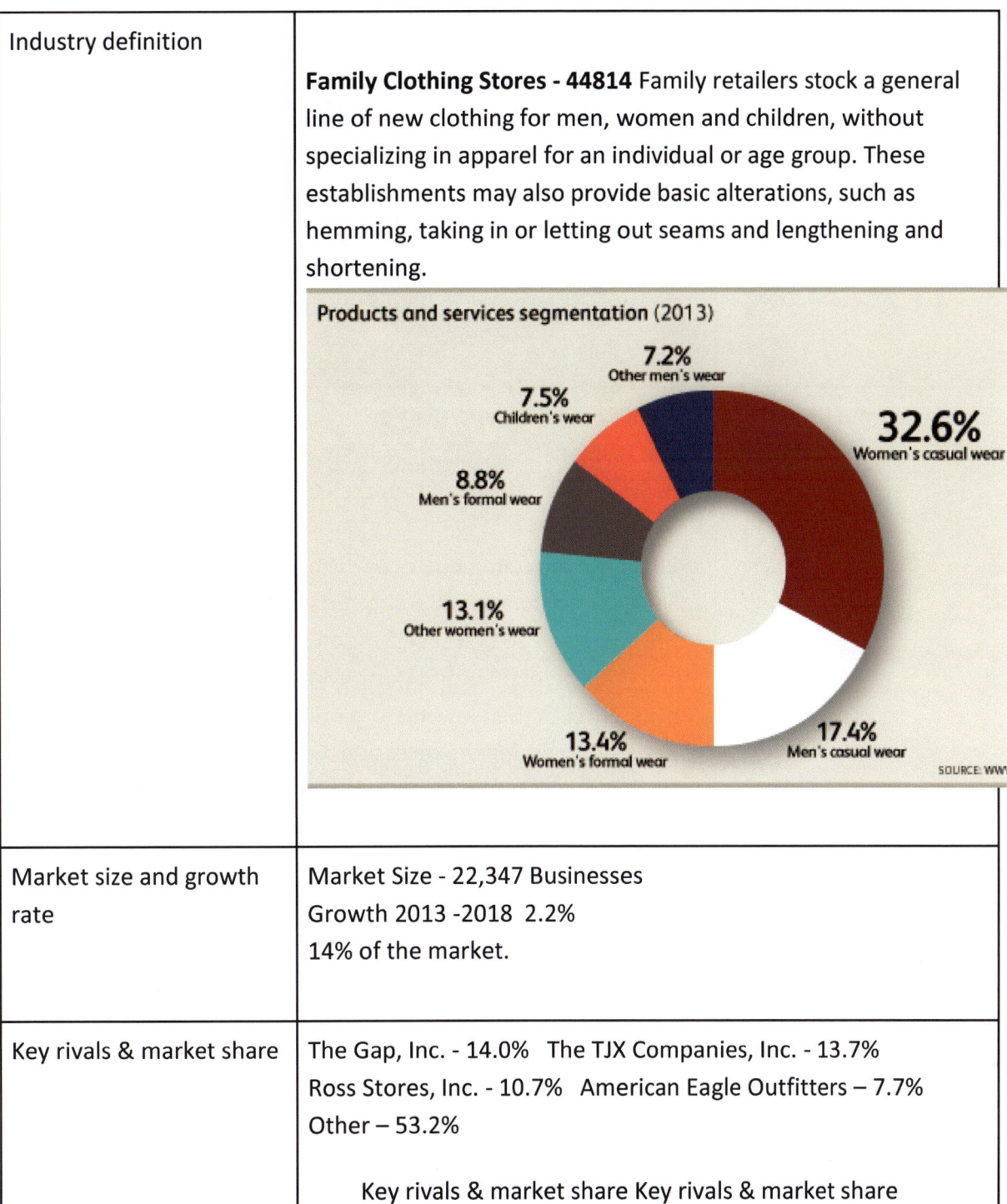
Market size and growth rate	Market Size - 22,347 Businesses Growth 2013 -2018 2.2% 14% of the market.
Key rivals & market share	The Gap, Inc. - 14.0% The TJX Companies, Inc. - 13.7% Ross Stores, Inc. - 10.7% American Eagle Outfitters – 7.7% Other – 53.2% Key rivals & market share Key rivals & market share

	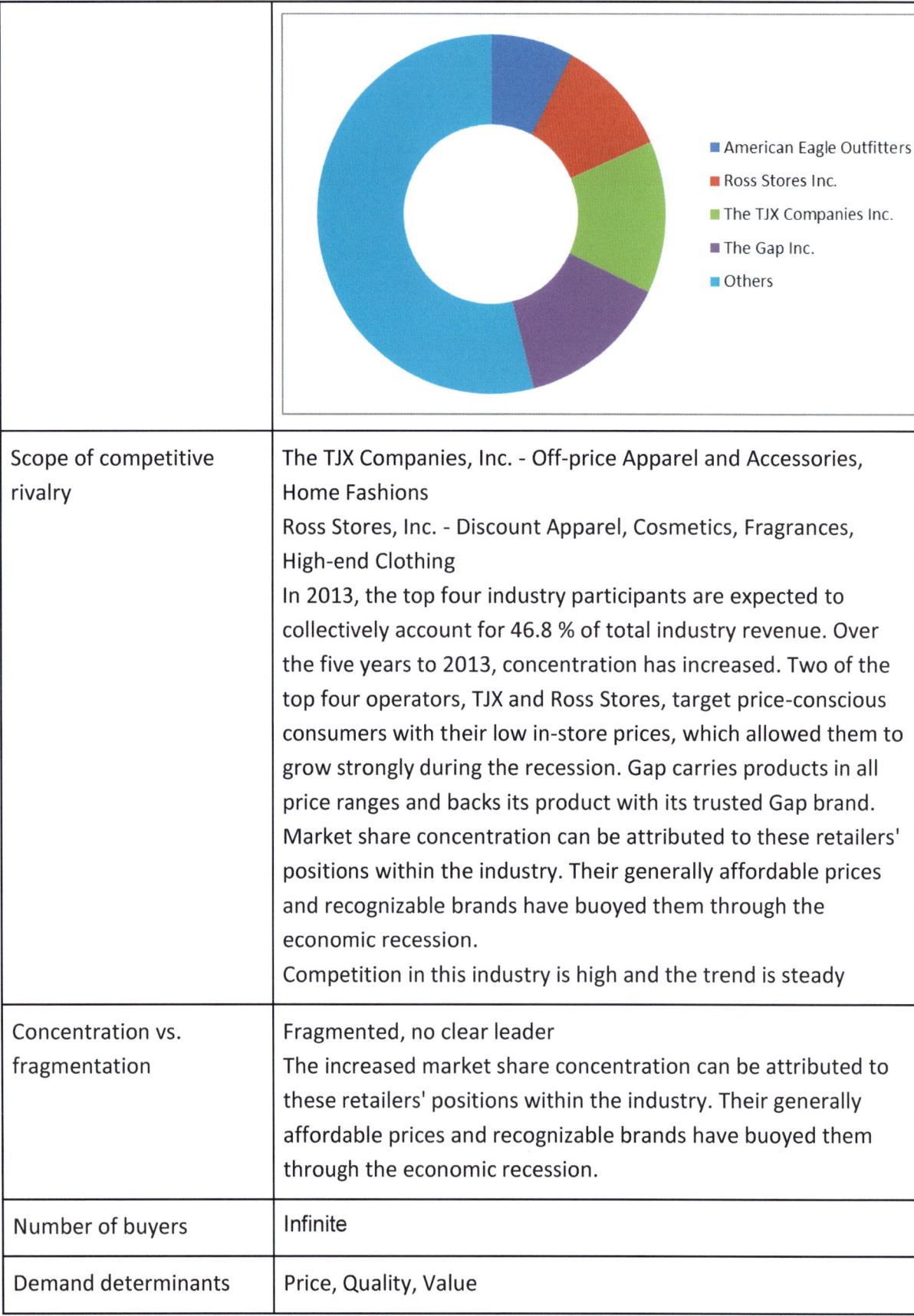
Scope of competitive rivalry	The TJX Companies, Inc. - Off-price Apparel and Accessories, Home Fashions Ross Stores, Inc. - Discount Apparel, Cosmetics, Fragrances, High-end Clothing In 2013, the top four industry participants are expected to collectively account for 46.8 % of total industry revenue. Over the five years to 2013, concentration has increased. Two of the top four operators, TJX and Ross Stores, target price-conscious consumers with their low in-store prices, which allowed them to grow strongly during the recession. Gap carries products in all price ranges and backs its product with its trusted Gap brand. Market share concentration can be attributed to these retailers' positions within the industry. Their generally affordable prices and recognizable brands have buoyed them through the economic recession. Competition in this industry is high and the trend is steady
Concentration vs. fragmentation	Fragmented, no clear leader The increased market share concentration can be attributed to these retailers' positions within the industry. Their generally affordable prices and recognizable brands have buoyed them through the economic recession.
Number of buyers	Infinite
Demand determinants	Price, Quality, Value

	The demand for family clothing is affected by a number of varying factors. Since clothing purchases within this industry are largely necessity-driven, price is an important determinant of demand. During the recession when consumer confidence and personal disposable income levels were low, Americans turned to lower-priced providers such as TJX and Ross Stores. Furthermore, the promotions and sales offered by family clothing stores can also affect demand. Households are likely to spend at stores that generate the most savings. Consumers' purchasing patterns are also guided by the strength and power of recognizable brand names. Brand perception may help retailers generate higher sales over their competitors.
Degree of product differentiation	Simple: based on a variety of characteristics, general line of clothing GAP Inc. has a clear market position projects a clear and consistent company image. They are also known for having their products stocked in line with current fashion trends and targeted to consumers' tastes.
Product innovation	Sustainable clothing, Moisture absorbent fabrics In order to spark product innovation GAP Inc. utilizes attractive product presentation; in which they provide a specific store layout and product display that must induce product purchase and reinforce the company's image.
Key success factors	Maintaining customer base, appealing style, product mix, value GAP Inc. key success factors include a quality of staff which has high energy to ensure excellent customer service. In addition, GAP Inc. has a clear market position which projects a clear and consistent company image. Last but not least, GAP Inc. has adequate stock control which is in place to reduce inventory costs and increase stock turns.
Supply/demand conditions	
	Erratic consumer buying, Product life cycles, Abundance of variety

	GAP Inc. Consumers' purchasing patterns are also guided by the strength and power of recognizable brand names. Brand perception may help retailers generate higher sales over their competitors. The largest operators within this industry are also the most recognizable: Gap Inc., TJX and Ross Stores. Fashion trends also influence sales to an extent, especially for retailers such as Abercrombie & Fitch. These stores focus on delivering a specific style of clothing to consumers, which cannot easily be found in competing retailers 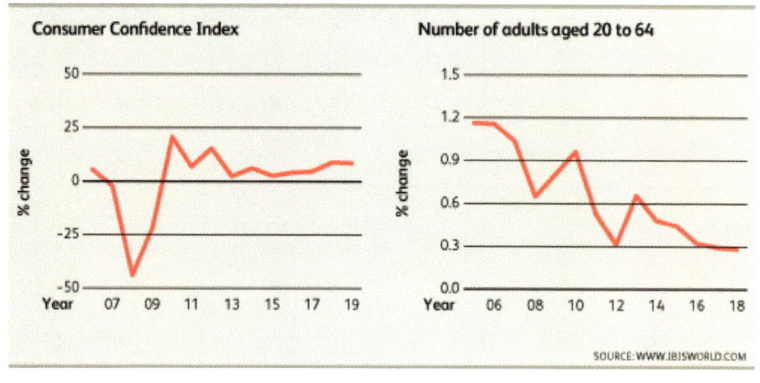
Analysis of stage in life cycle	Mature As part of a fairly established sector and with few opportunities to expand, the Family Clothing Stores industry continues to operate in the mature stage of its life cycle. Its industry value added (IVA), which measures the industry's contribution to the economy, is expected to grow 6.4% per year on average over the 10 years to 2018, compared with GDP growth of 2.1% per year on average. IVA is anticipated to outpace general economic growth because of the industry's weak performance during the recession. Profit and wages, two of the components of IVA, along with depreciation, plummeted in 2008 and 2009. Since then, the industry has made vast improvements and is expected to continue in this fashion over the next five years, which contributes to its strong IVA growth. The growth of family apparel stores has saturated the market. The Industry value added is expected to outperform overall economic growth primarily due to a rebound in wages and profit

	over the next five years 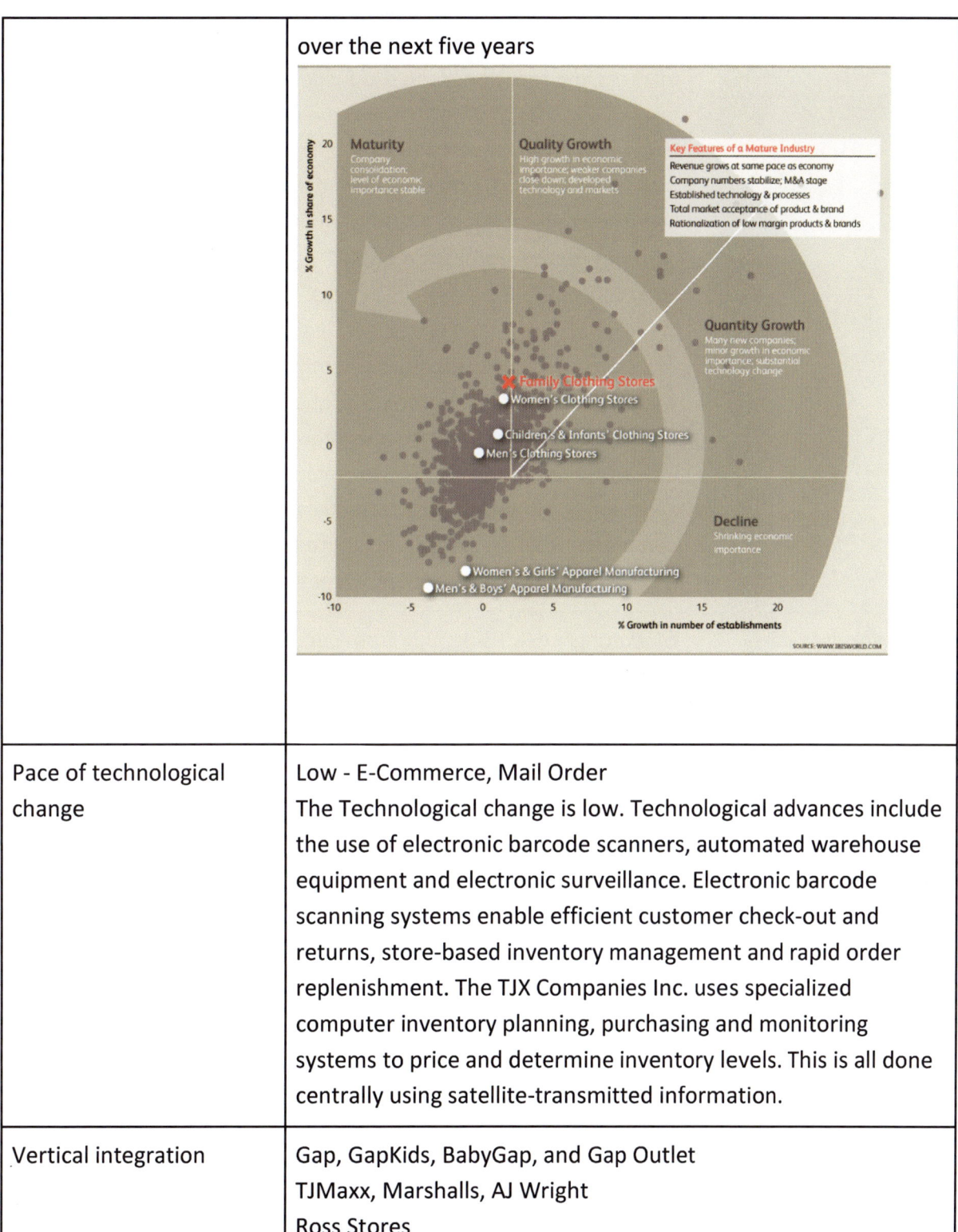
Pace of technological change	Low - E-Commerce, Mail Order The Technological change is low. Technological advances include the use of electronic barcode scanners, automated warehouse equipment and electronic surveillance. Electronic barcode scanning systems enable efficient customer check-out and returns, store-based inventory management and rapid order replenishment. The TJX Companies Inc. uses specialized computer inventory planning, purchasing and monitoring systems to price and determine inventory levels. This is all done centrally using satellite-transmitted information.
Vertical integration	Gap, GapKids, BabyGap, and Gap Outlet TJMaxx, Marshalls, AJ Wright Ross Stores American Eagle GAP Inc., industry players must differentiate themselves from the competition, both within and outside the Family Clothing

	Stores industry. Retailers will likely move into less-tapped markets and focus on niche products, like plus-sized clothing or fashion-forward apparel, to continue expanding. Brand- and image-sensitive shoppers of the Generation Y market will increasingly look to designs that showcase a unique style, so apparel retailers will increasingly alter product lines to keep up with this demographic. External competition, specifically from specialty men's, women's and children's clothing stores, will likely intensify over the next five years. Operators within the Family Clothing Stores industry will compete on the basis of style, quality and, to a much lesser extent, price. By anticipating customer-preferred trends, industry retailers will be able to stock their inventories accordingly. However, this strategy can be unprofitable if competing retailers better anticipate these trends or have a larger selection of products for target consumers.
Economies of scale	Marketing/Advertising, Buy from overseas manufacturers GAP, Inc. economies of scale include a quality of staff which has high energy to ensure excellent customer service. In addition, GAP, Inc. has a clear market position which projects a clear and consistent company image. Last but not least, GAP, Inc. has adequate stock control which is in place to reduce inventory costs and increase stock turns.
Learning/experience curve effects	The world price of cotton is expected to continue its upward trend over the next five years. As a result, apparel manufacturers will attempt to pass on the increasing price of cotton, which will put pressure on retailers' purchasing costs. Growing imports may offer some relief, however, as apparel retailers will be able to save on purchase costs from inexpensive imported products. IBIS World forecasts that imports will make up an increasing share of domestic demand for clothing, with import penetration at the manufacturing level expanding through 2018 and satisfying 31.5% of domestic demand. Within the clothing manufacturing sector, imports' share of domestic demand will be even higher, reaching 98.2% for the Men's and Boys' Apparel Manufacturing industry and 78.6% for the

	Women's and Girls' Apparel Manufacturing industry. Because most imported apparel is more affordable than domestically made clothing, inventory costs for family clothing stores will be lower. Meanwhile, increased domestic demand for clothes will allow retailers to return to prerecession price points. Together, these trends will increase profit margins (i.e. earnings before interest and tax) for family clothing stores, from an estimated 7.6% of revenue in 2013 to 9.7% by 2018.
Barriers to entry	Medium Barriers to entry for the clothing industry are considered medium and steady. The high costs involved in developing and maintaining brand reputations provide a major barrier to entry in this industry. As existing players have already established brand names in respective product offerings, new entrants will have to invest money and time before consumers shift away from strong brand names and purchase relatively new brands. Due to the recent economic slowdown, consumer demand has shifted toward more competitively priced clothing. Family clothing stores have catered to these demands by providing branded merchandise at discounted prices. Existing stores, such as TJX and Ross Stores, are able to offer merchandise at discounted prices by purchasing products earlier in the season at low prices through established sourcing networks. **Barriers to Entry checklist** — **Level** Competition — High Concentration — Medium Life Cycle Stage — Mature Capital Intensity — Medium Technology Change — Low Regulation & Policy — Medium Industry Assistance — Low SOURCE: WWW.IBISWORLD.COM
Regulation/deregulation	Is considered medium within the family clothing industry.
Globalization	Globalization in this industry is low and the trend is steady. The

	Family Clothing Stores industry is comprised of a large number of small companies; over 80.0% of firms operating within the industry employ four or fewer people, so no single company owns a substantial portion of the market. Additionally, the major companies in this industry are all domestically owned. However, the Gap generates about 12.0% of its total revenue from international markets and the TJX Corporation generates about 15.0% of its sales from international markets. These numbers are still relatively small compared with overall revenue, giving the industry a low level of globalization.
Trends	Good quality at a low price, value In the industry of Family Clothing they are rapidly expanding E-Commerce and Online Auctions industry. Online-only stores offer consumers the ease of shopping at home, since individuals can search for specific items and compare prices with the click of a button. In a price-sensitive environment, consumers have been especially interested in finding the best deals on their purchases. These advantages give e-tailers a competitive edge over traditional brick-and-mortar family clothing stores.

Organization Structure

The Gap, Inc. is a Multidivisional Structure it is based on global strategy. The Gap, Inc. announced in a Press Release a new global brand structure designed to fuel the company's long-term growth. Gap Inc.'s five brands and over 3,200 stores are currently located in more than 40 countries worldwide, up from just eight countries in 2006. The company will bring together its North American, International, Online, Outlet and Franchise divisions under a single global executive for each of its Gap, Banana Republic and Old Navy brands.

In addition, to build upon the company's considerable online success and industry-leading technological advances, the company will form a new Innovation and Digital Strategy team to further its leadership position in this area. Looking forward we are anticipating the following:

- Long-term growth, gaining market share, and enhancing shareholder value;
- Expected management changes;
- Building upon success in North America and in e-commerce;
- Additional investments to build digital capabilities;

- Significant long-term opportunity in China; and
- Expected online sales levels and timing.

The risk that changes in general economic conditions or consumer spending patterns could adversely impact the company's results of operations;

- the highly competitive nature of the company's business in the United States and internationally;
- the risk that the company or its franchisees will be unsuccessful in gauging apparel trends and changing consumer preferences;
- the risk that the company's franchisees will be unable to successfully open, operate, and grow their franchised stores in a manner consistent with the company's requirements regarding its brand identities and customer experience standards;
- the risk that the company or its franchisees will be unsuccessful in identifying, negotiating, and securing new store locations and renewing, modifying or terminating leases for existing store locations effectively;
- the risk that comparable sales and margins will experience fluctuations;
- the risk that updates or changes to the company's information technology ("IT") systems may disrupt its operations;
- the risk that natural disasters, public health crises, political crises, or other catastrophic events could adversely affect the company's operations and financial results;

- the risk that acts or omissions by the company's third-party vendors, including a failure to comply with the company's code of vendor conduct, could have a negative impact on its reputation or operations;
- the risk that the company will not be successful in defending various proceedings, lawsuits, disputes, claims, and audits; and
- the risk that changes in the regulatory or administrative landscape could adversely affect the company's financial condition, strategies, and results of operations.

Press Release, "Gap Inc. Creates Global Brand Management Structure to Drive the Company's Long-Term Growth", SAN FRANCISCO – October 16, 2012

The Gap, Inc. uses related diversification to create a global brand through complementary businesses. They are related through market, customer groups, product lines, geographic regions and technology. Most product offerings are designed by us and manufactured by independent sources. They also sell products that are designed that are designed and manufactured by branded third parties.

The Gap, Inc. is using a Decentralized Organizational Structure where each brand has its own leadership and decision-making authority. They will draw on the combined intellectual capital of all its employees.

Advantages
- Creates new ideas and creative thinking
- Prompt response times to market changes
- Will have fewer layers of management
- Empower employees to be resourceful and act responsibly

Disadvantages
- Top management may be unaware of actions taken by empowered personnel
- Puts organization at risk if empowered employees make bad business choices
- May reduce cross-unit participation

Financial Analysis

Key Financial Ratios- The Gap			
	2010	2011	2012
Profitability Ratios			
Gross Profit Margin	40%	37%	39%
Operating Profit Margin	14%	10%	12%
Net Profit Margin	8%	6%	7%
Return on total Assets	16%	13%	17%
Return on Stockholder's Equity	27%	25%	40%
Return on invested capital	27%	21%	28%
Earnings Per Share	13%	6%	6%
Liquidity Ratios			
Current Ratio	1.9	2.0	1.8
Working Capital	1831	2181	1788
Leverage Ratios			
Debt to asset	0.4	0.6	0.4
Debt to equity	0.7	1.6	1.5
Long Term Debt to Equity	0.0	0.6	0.4
Activity Ratios			
Days of Inventory	69.0	68.3	69.8
Average Collection Period	5.1	7.5	7.7
Inventory turnover	5.2	5.3	5.3
Total Asset Turnover	2.2	2.0	2.2
Other			
Dividend Payout	20.9	28.3	21.2
Operating Expenses/Net Sales	86%	90%	88%
COGS/Net Sales	55%	59%	57%
SG&A/Net Sales	27%	26%	57%

Key Financial Ratios-TJX			
	2010	2011	2012
Profitability Ratios			
Gross Profit Margin	27%	27%	28%
Operating Profit Margin	10%	11%	12%
Net Profit Margin	6%	6%	7%
Return on total Assets	18%	19%	22%
Return on Stockholder's Equity	45%	47%	55%
Return on invested capital	36%	39%	46%
Earnings Per Share	6%	5%	4%
Liquidity Ratios			
Current Ratio	1.6	1.7	1.5
Working Capital	1967	2070	1951
Leverage Ratios			
Debt to asset	0.6	0.6	0.6
Debt to equity	1.6	1.6	1.6
Long Term Debt to Equity	0.3	0.2	0.2
Activity Ratios			
Days of Inventory	62.1	63.7	60.4
Average Collection Period	3.3	3.2	3.1
Inventory turnover	5.6	5.5	6.0
Other			
Dividend Payout	17.8	18.1	17.6
Operating Expenses/Net Sales	90.0%	89.5%	88.0%
COGS/Net Sales	71%	71%	70%
SG&A/Net Sales	17%	17%	16%

Key Financial Ratios-Ross			
	2010	2011	2012
Profitability Ratios			
Gross Profit Margin	27%	28%	28%
Operating Profit Margin	12%	12%	13%
Net Profit Margin	7%	8%	8%
Return on total Assets	19%	21%	23%
Return on Stockholder's Equity	45%	47%	48%
Return on invested capital	40%	43%	44%
Earnings Per Share	5%	6%	5%
Liquidity Ratios			
Current Ratio	1.5	1.4	1.4
Working Capital	691	578	608
Leverage Ratios			
Debt to asset	0.6	0.5	0.5
Debt to equity	1.3	1.2	1.1
Long Term Debt to Equity	0.1	0.1	0.1
Activity Ratios			
Days of Inventory	64.2	66.5	62.5
Average Collection Period	2.1	2.2	2.3
Total Asset Turnover	2.5	2.6	2.7
Inventory turnover	5.7	5.5	5.8
Other			
Dividend Payout	14.2	14.6	14.9
Operating Expenses/Net Sales	88%	88%	87%
COGS/Net Sales	71%	71%	70%
SG&A/Net Sales	16%	15%	15%

Key Financial Ratios-American Eagle			
	2010	2011	2012
Profitability Ratios			
Gross Profit Margin	40%	31%	44%
Operating Profit Margin	8%	8%	20%
Net Profit Margin	6%	5%	7%
Return on total Assets	7%	8%	13%
Return on Stockholder's Equity	9%	11%	18%
Return on Invested Capital	9%	11%	18%
Earnings Per Share		5%	6%
Liquidity Ratios			
Current Ratio	3.0	3.2	2.6
Working Capital	786	882	706
Leverage Ratios			
Debt to asset	0.3	0.3	0.3
Debt to equity	0.4	0.4	0.4
Long Term Debt to Equity	0.0	0.0	0.0
Activity Ratios			
Days of Inventory		61.1	70.8
Average Collection Period	4.6	4.6	4.8
Inventory turnover	6.0	6.0	5.2
Other			
Operating Expenses/Net Sales	93%	92%	80%
COGS/Net Sales	67%	64%	53%
SG&A/Net Sales	25%	23%	24%

Revenue Comparison 2010-2012

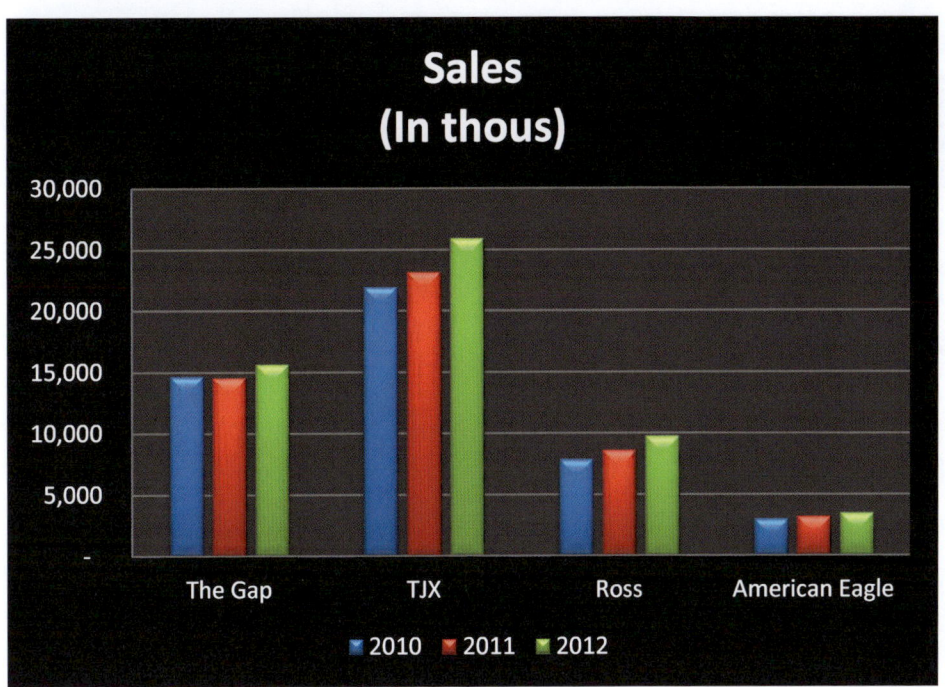

Sales	2010	2011	2012	% increase from 2010 to 2012
The Gap	14,664	14,549	15,651	7%
TJX	21,942	23,191	25,878	18%
Ross	7,866	8,608	9,721	24%
American Eagle	2,968	3,160	3,476	17%

Gap sales have only increased 7% from 2010 to 2012. On the other hand, its competitor's sales have increased drastically, despite the economic recession. TJX, Ross, and American Eagle, have increased their sales by more than half and triple.

Net Income Comparison 2010-2012

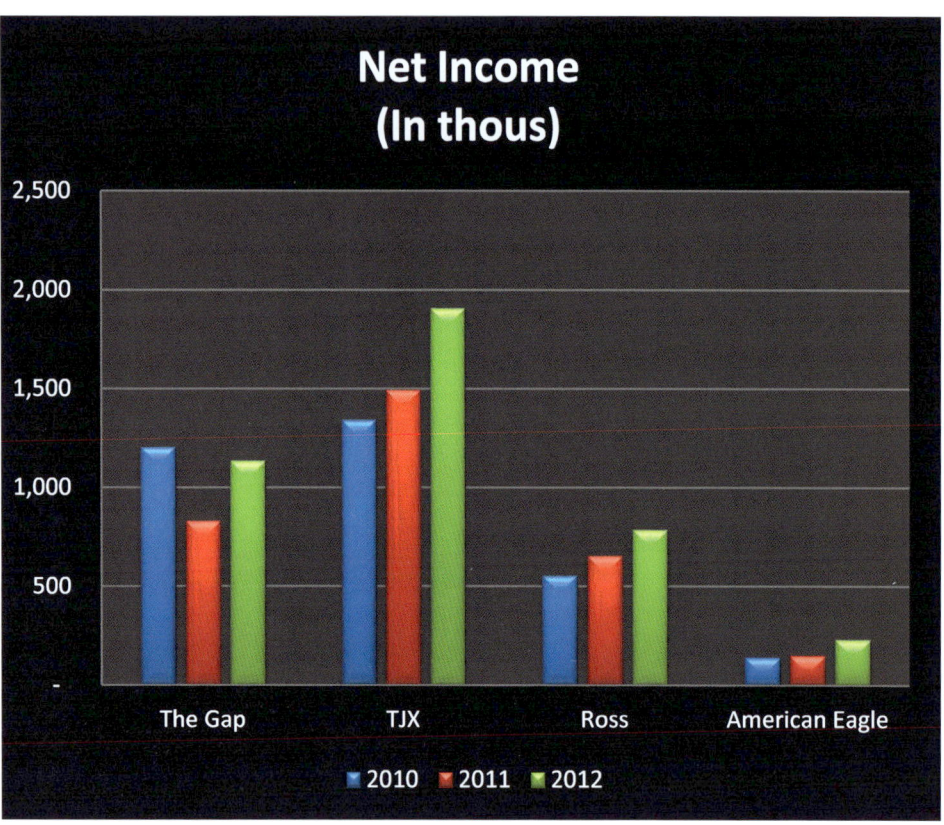

Net Income	2010	2011	2012	% increase from 2010 to 2012
The Gap	1,204	833	1,135	-6%
TJX	1,343	1,496	1,907	42%
Ross	555	657	787	42%
American Eagle	141	152	232	65%

During the past 3 years, Gap income's has decreased by 6%, while its competitors have increased drastically.

Gross Profit Margin Comparison 2010-2012

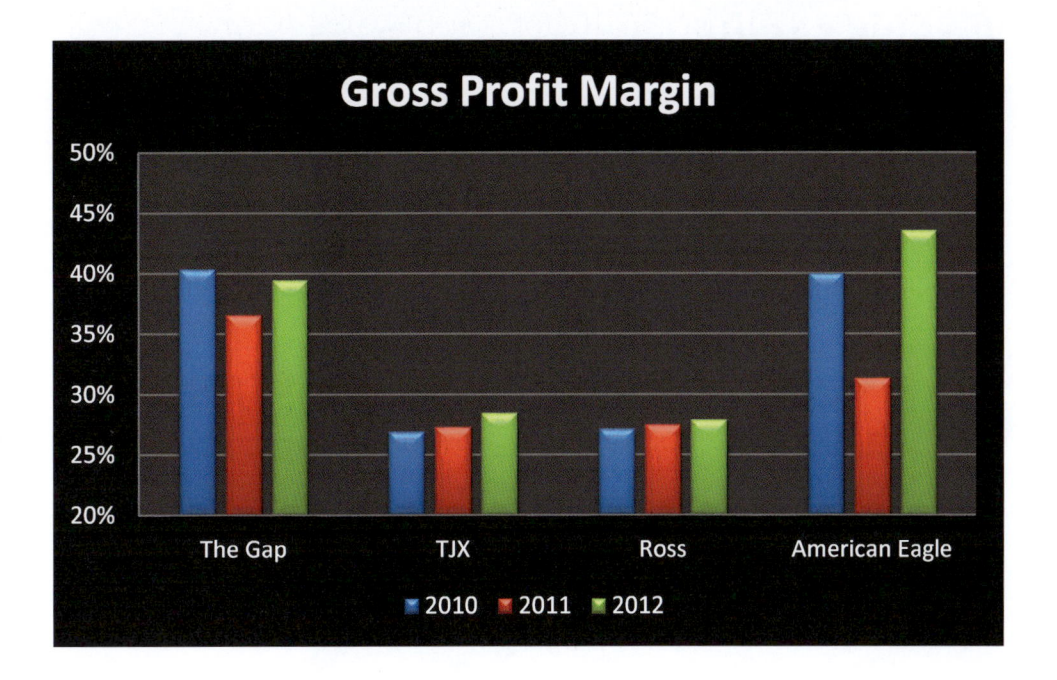

Gross Profit Margin

Gross Profit Margin	2010	2011	2012
The Gap	40%	37%	39%
TJX	27%	27%	28%
Ross	27%	28%	28%
American Eagle	40%	31%	44%

Gap has the strongest gross profit margin when comparing it to TJX and Ross. However, American Eagle has the strongest gross profit margin among the four stores. Despite, the slight decrease of gross profit margin from 2010 to 2012, Gap shows a relatively strong gross profit margin. This is a great indication that Gap has the ability to pay additional expenses not planned for if needed in the future.

Operating Profit Margin Comparison 2010-2012

Operating Profit Margin	2010	2011	2012
The Gap	14%	10%	12%
TJX	10%	11%	12%
Ross	12%	12%	13%
American Eagle	8%	8%	20%

Return on Total Assets Comparison 2010-2012

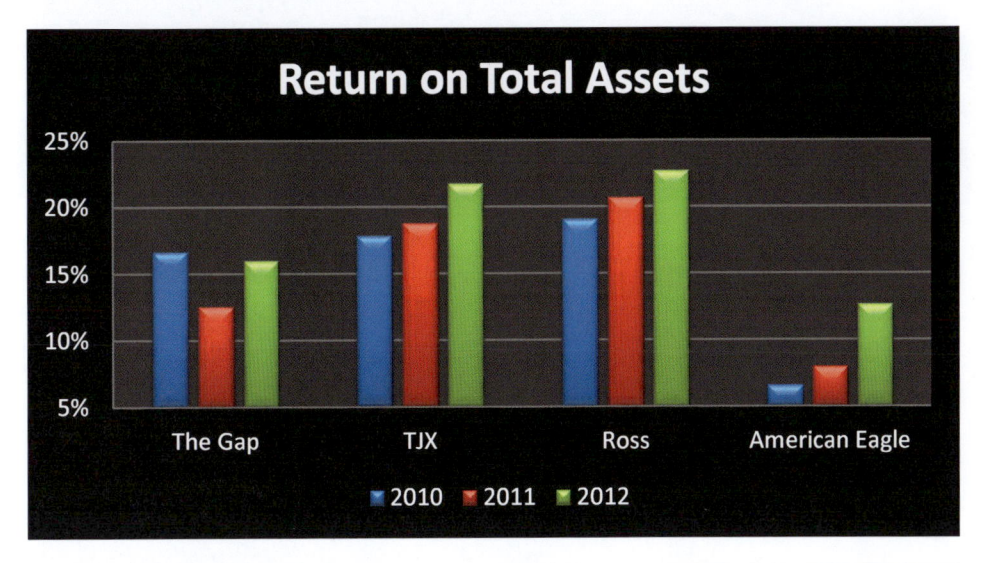

Return on Total Assets

Return on Total Assets	2010	2011	2012
The Gap	17%	13%	16%
TJX	18%	19%	22%
Ross	19%	21%	23%
American Eagle	7%	8%	13%

Gap's Return on Total Assets decreased by 4% from 2010 to 2011 and increased by 3% from 2011 to 2011. The increase is an indication that in 2012 Gap was able to better utilize its assets for profitability. However, two of its competitors, TJX and Ross, have a higher Return on Assets than Gap. It is evident that TJX and Ross are more efficiently using its assets to increase profitability.

Return on Stockholder's Equity Comparison 2010-2012

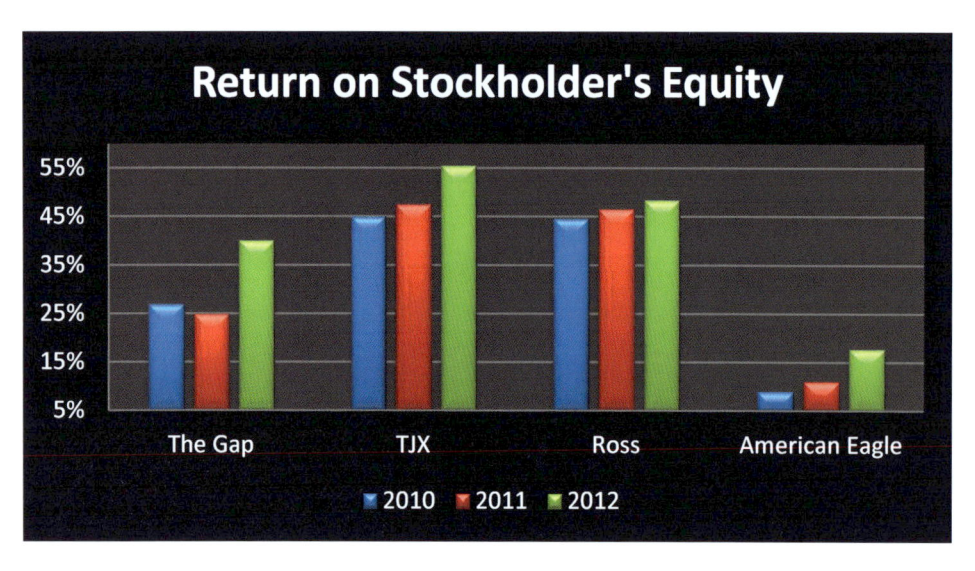

Return on Stockholder's Equity

Return on Stockholder's Equity	2010	2011	2012
The Gap	27%	25%	39%
TJX	45%	47%	55%
Ross	45%	47%	48%
American Eagle	9%	11%	18%

Gap and its competitors ROE increased from 2010 to 2012. However, The Gap has the lowest Return on Stockholder's Equity when comparing it to TJX and Ross. In 2012, Gap's Return on Stockholder's Equity was 39%, while TJX was 55%, and Ross, 48%. This reflects that Gap is not maximizing its sales, asset turnover, and financial leverage in comparison to its competitors.

Current Ratio Comparison 2010-2012

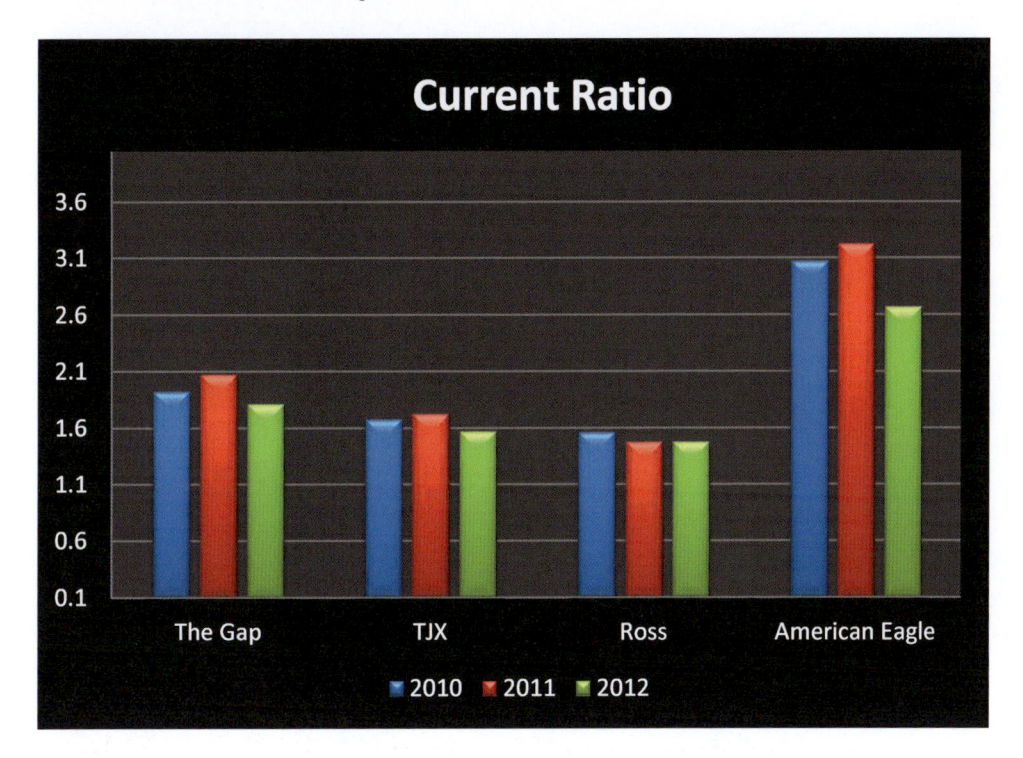

Current Ratio

Current Ratio	2010	2011	2012
The Gap	1.9	2.0	1.8
TJX	1.6	1.7	1.5
Ross	1.5	1.4	1.4
American Eagle	3.0	3.2	2.6

All four companies do not show a current ratio of less than one. This is an indication that all the companies have the capability to pay off short term obligations. The Gap's current ratio is the highest when comparing it to TJX and Ross.

Debt to Asset Ratio Comparison 2010-2012

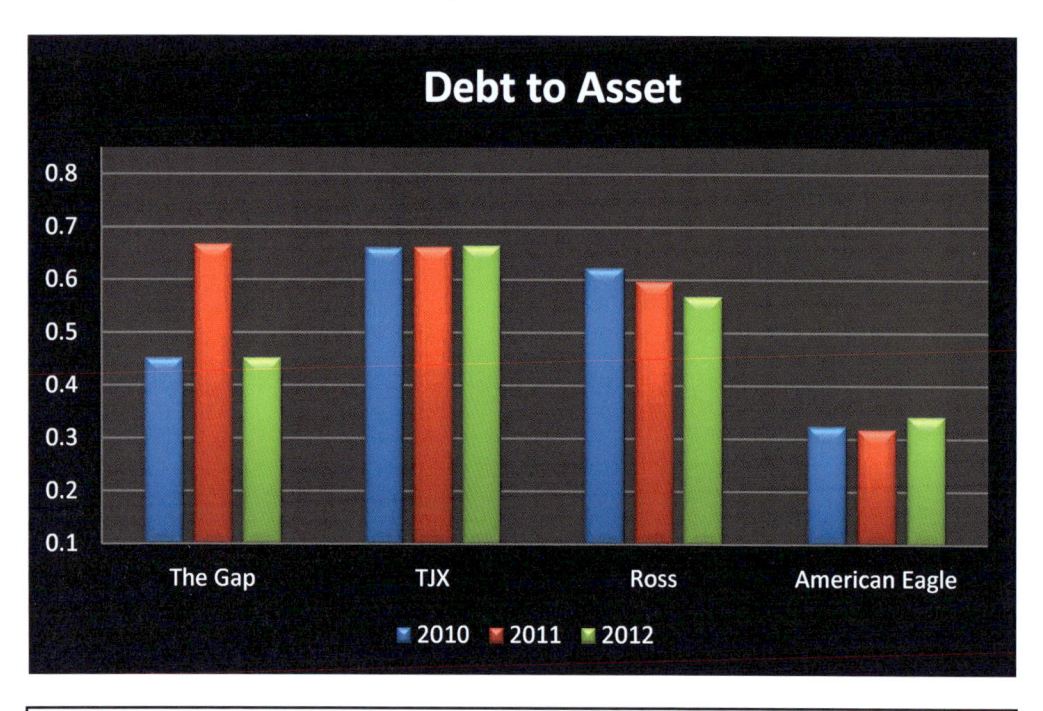

Debt to Asset

Debt to Asset	2010	2011	2012
The Gap	0.4	0.6	0.4
TJX	0.6	0.6	0.6
Ross	0.6	0.5	0.5
American Eagle	0.3	0.3	0.3

In 2012, The Gap has almost the lowest Debt to Asset ratio when comparing it to its competitors. American Eagle is the only company with a lower ratio of .3. From 2010 to 2012, the Gap debt to asset ratio increased and then decreased in 2012. Overall, The Gap debt to asset ratio positively impacts the company in the future because this illustrates that there is no overuse of debt, therefore a low risk of bankruptcy.

Inventory Turnover Ratio Comparison 2010-2012

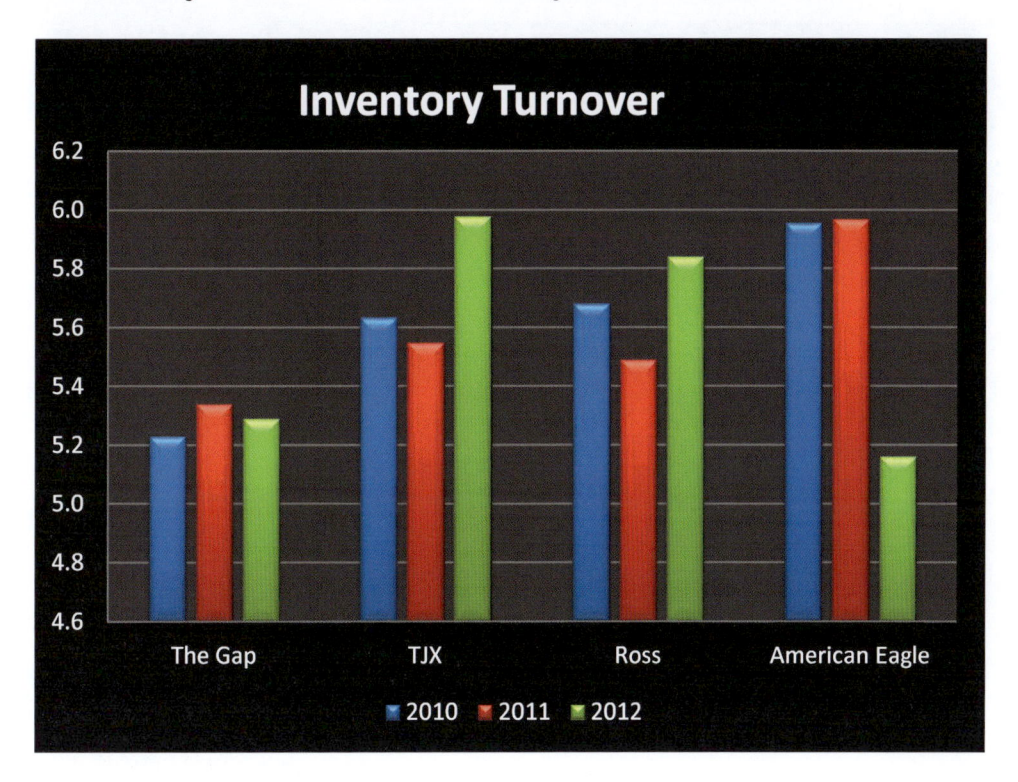

Inventory Turnover

Inventory Turnover	2010	2011	2012
The Gap	5.2	5.3	5.3
TJX	5.6	5.5	6.0
Ross	5.7	5.5	5.8
American Eagle	6.0	6.0	5.2

The Gap's inventory turnover ratio has increased only by 1% from 2010 to 2012. Its competitors have higher ratios. This is an indication that The Gap needs to increase its inventory turnover ratio. The Gap needs to sell its inventory more efficiently. The By doing so, The Gap will minimize inventory holdings leading to a reduction in overhead costs. As a result, it will improve the profitability of the company.

COGS/Sales % Comparison 2010-2012

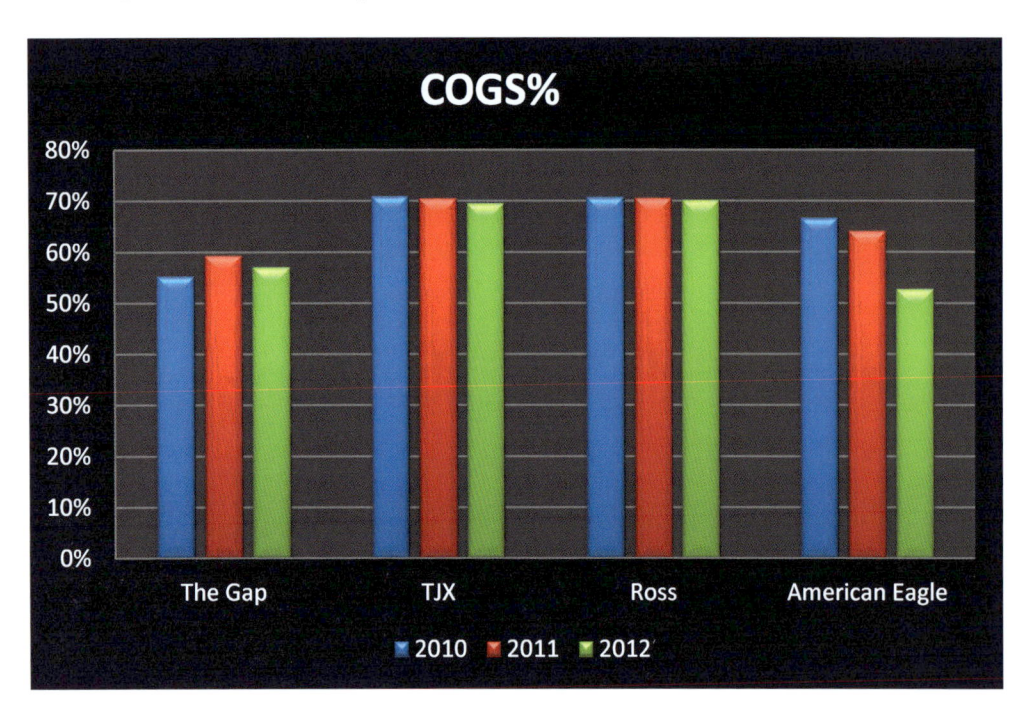

COGS%

COGS%	2010	2011	2012
The Gap	55%	59%	57%
TJX	71%	71%	70%
Ross	71%	71%	70%
American Eagle	67%	64%	53%

In 2010 and 2011, Gap's cost of goods sold percentage over sales was lower than its competitors. However, in 2012, American Eagle's cost of goods sold percentage over sales was lower, 53% and Gap was higher, 57%. Overall, Gap is more favorable when comparing with its competitors because the lower ratio indicates that it is earning more revenue on each sale. From 2011 to 2012, Gap's percentage decreased by 2%, which is an indication of profitability.

SG&A/Sales % Comparison 2010-2012

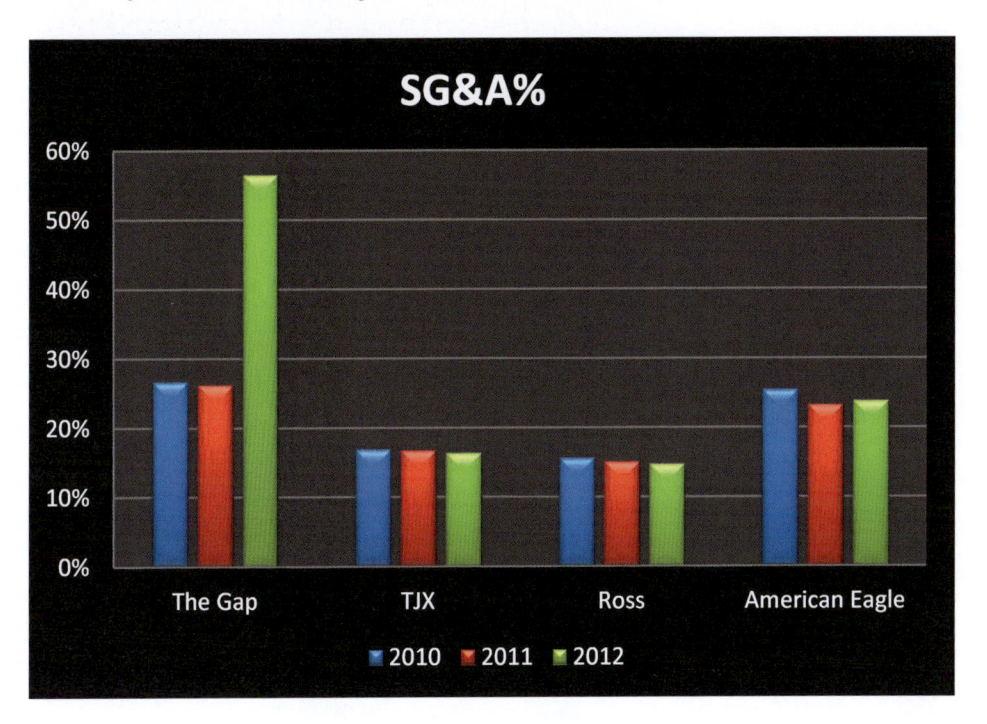

SG&A%

SG&A%	2010	2011	2012
The Gap	27%	26%	57%
TJX	17%	17%	16%
Ross	16%	15%	15%
American Eagle	25%	23%	24%

Gap has the highest selling general administrative expenses to sales ratio when comparing it with its competitors. From 2011 to 2012, it also drastically increased by 21%. This negatively impacts Gap because it is evident that there is very high spending. This leads to questioning whether management are spending efficiently or wasting valuable cash flow. Gap management should reevaluate the SG& A expenses to reduce some costs.

Altman

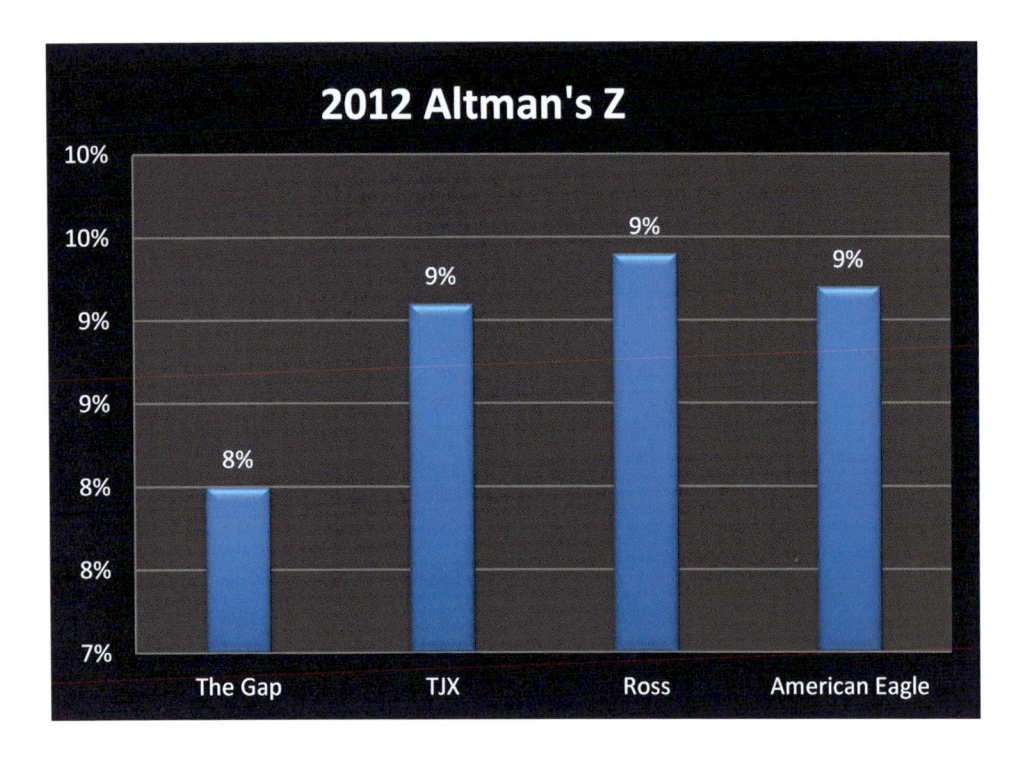

2012 Altman's Z

Company	Score
The Gap	8%
TJX	9%
Ross	9%
American Eagle	9%

- Score above 3.0 is an indication that the company is safe.
- Score between 2.7 and 2.99 is an indication that the company should exercise caution
- Score between 1.8 and 2.7 is an indication the company has a chance of the going bankruptcy within 2 years of operations from the date of the financial figures presented.

Ultimately, the Altman Z-Score helps investors determine the probability of a company going bankrupt. Overall all four companies scored 8% and above which portrays to investors the companies are safe based on the financial figures.

Tobin's Q

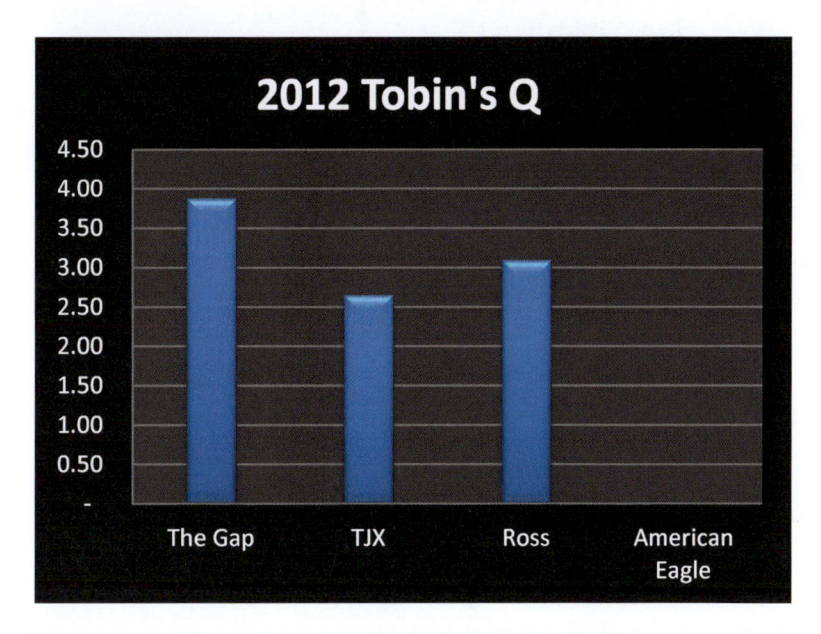

2012 Tobin's Q

Tobin's Q	Mkt Value- Apr 2	Book Value	%
The Gap	41.89	10.82	3.87
TJX	62.16	23.44	2.65
Ross	73.50	23.80	3.09
American Eagle	12.72	-	-

In 2012, Gap has the highest ratio within its competitors and is greater than 1. This implies that the firm's stock is more expensive than the replacement cost of its assets. In other words, the stock is overvalued.

DuPont Analysis

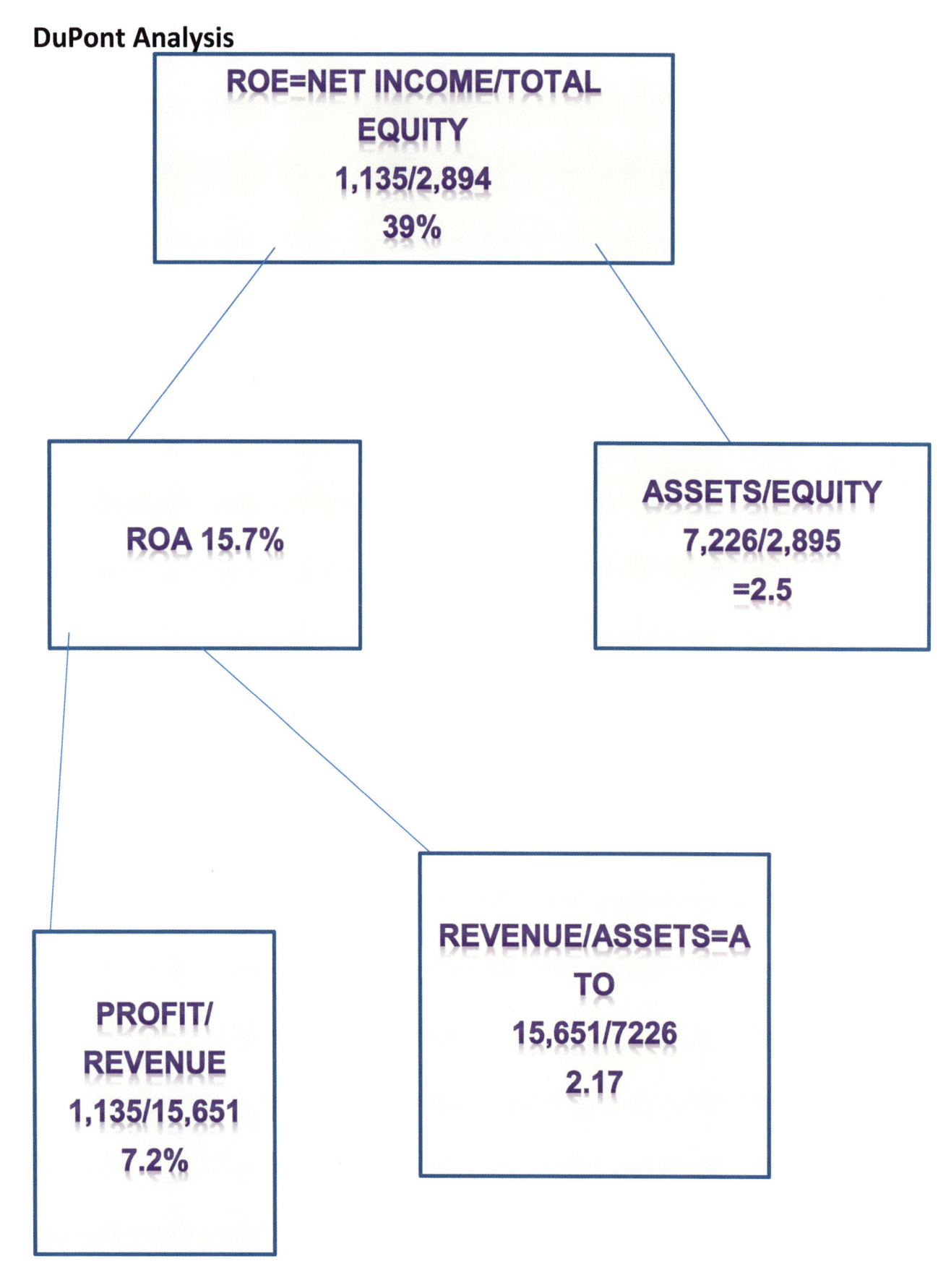

```
┌─────────────────────────────┐
│ ROE=NET INCOME/TOTAL EQUITY │
│         1,135/2,894         │
│             39%             │
└─────────────────────────────┘
         /              \
        /                \
┌───────────────┐   ┌──────────────────┐
│   ROA 15.7%   │   │  ASSETS/EQUITY   │
│               │   │   7,226/2,895    │
│               │   │      =2.5        │
└───────────────┘   └──────────────────┘
     /        \
    /          \
┌──────────────┐  ┌──────────────────────┐
│   PROFIT/    │  │ REVENUE/ASSETS=A TO  │
│   REVENUE    │  │      15,651/7226     │
│ 1,135/15,651 │  │         2.17         │
│     7.2%     │  │                      │
└──────────────┘  └──────────────────────┘
```

Stock Analysis

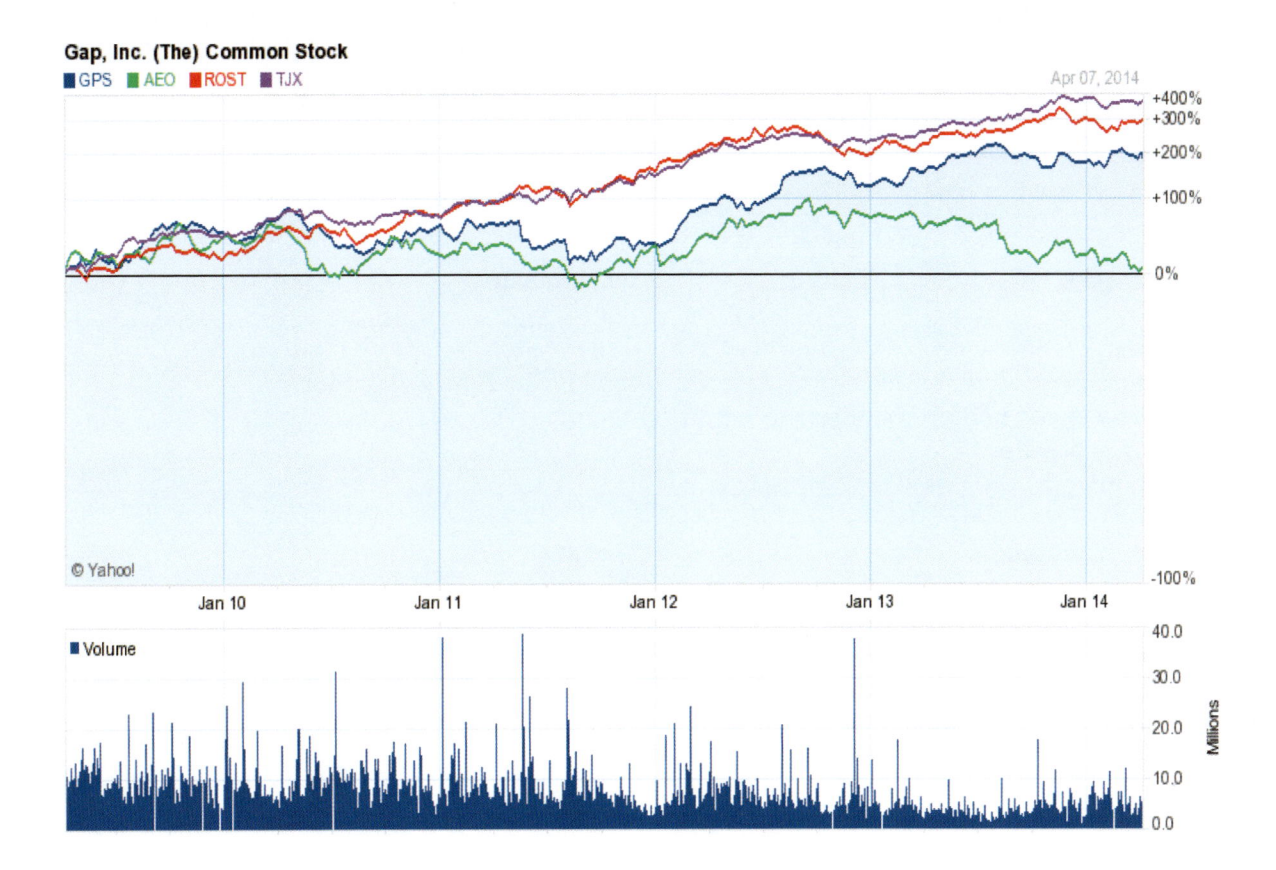

SWOT Analysis

Gap is a specialty retailer offering apparel, accessories and personal care products for men, women, children and babies under the Gap, Old Navy, Banana Republic, Piperlime, Athleta and Intermix brand names. The company enjoys a wide geographic presence with operations spread across various countries. Widespread presence diversifies Gap's business risk and also increases its addressable market. However, increasing labor costs could increase the company's operating cost and adversely affect its margins.

Strengths	Weaknesses
Global presence catalyzed by franchise and company-owned stores and online presence	Dependence on outside merchandise vendors for supply of products
Well balanced portfolio of value as well as upscale brands	
High margins compared to competitors	

Opportunities	Threats
Growing e-commerce market	Increasing labor costs
Growing apparel industry	Growing market for counterfeit products
Expansion into the growing luxury retail market	
Expanding presence in Asian markets	

Strengths
Global presence catalyzed by franchise and company-owned stores and online presence

Over the years, Gap has built a wide geographic presence with operations across various countries. Gap primarily operates through company-owned stores, various franchise agreements and online retail websites. It also operates outlet retail stores for the Gap and Banana Republic brands. Gap runs its company-owned stores in the US, Canada, the UK, France, Ireland, Japan, China and Italy. At the end of FY2013, the company had 3,095 company-owned retail stores. Gap also has various franchise agreements with unaffiliated franchisees to operate Gap and Banana Republic stores throughout Asia, Australia, Eastern Europe, Latin America, the Middle East, and Africa. Under these franchise agreements, third parties operate stores that sell apparel and related products under the company's brand names. In FY2013, Gap had 312 franchise stores in 40 countries. Though franchise stores are a small part of the company's business, they play an important role in aiding Gap's efforts to expand internationally.

Apart from the brick and mortar format, Gap also has presence in various countries through its online retail websites. The company began online operations of its Gap brand in 1997. The online retail websites for Banana Republic and Old Navy were launched for the US market in 1999 and 2000, respectively. Additionally, in 2010, the online retail facility for the brands Gap, Banana Republic and Old Navy was also made available in Canada, the UK and some other

European nations. The company also has an online store for the Piperlime brand. Beginning from 2010, Piperlime was made available in other select international countries. Athleta branded products are also available for sale through the online retail platform. Gap has been growing its online presence in various European nations, North America as well as many developing nations in the Asia-Pacific region. Gap launched an online retail store in China, www.gap.cn, in 2010. In the following year, the company launched e-commerce sites for eight European countries, including Austria, Estonia, Finland, Malta, Luxembourg, Portugal, Slovakia and Slovenia. Expanding its international presence further, in October 2012, Gap launched its online stores (gap.co.jp and bananarepublic.co.jp) in Japan. Currently, Gap products are available to customers online in over 80 countries. In FY2013, the direct segment's sales increased by 23.5% over FY2012. The company's three pronged strategy has allowed it to expand into various geographies. Widespread presence broadens the company's customer base and diversifies business risk by decreasing dependence on mature markets such as the US and the UK.

Well balanced portfolio of value as well as upscale brands
Gap has a well balanced portfolio of brands that helps the company to cater to separate groups of target customers including those who seek value or upscale brands or both. The company's brands Gap, Banana Republic and Piperlime cater to the high end customer segment. The Gap brand offers an extensive range of classically styled, casual apparel at moderate price points. The company also operates Gap Outlet stores. These stores offer similar categories of products as offered by the Gap brand, however at lower price points. The Banana Republic brand offers fashionable collection of casual and tailored apparel, shoes, accessories and personal care products for men and women at price points higher than the Gap brand. The company also operates Banana Republic Factory Stores, which offer similar categories of products as Banana Republic, however, at lower price points. Additionally, the Piperlime brand offers an assortment of the national brands in the categories of footwear, handbags, apparel, and jewelry for women and footwear for men and kids. The company also offers women's sports and active apparel and footwear under the brand name Athleta. Furthermore, Gap offers luxury and contemporary fashion and designer brands through the Intermix brand, which was acquired in December 2012. Gap's presence in the value apparel and accessories market is represented by its offerings under the brand name Old Navy. Old Navy is positioned as a value priced family apparel retailer. Across every department, Old Navy ensured that merchandise decisions were made with target family audience. As a result, the brand has been able to deliver fashion at value prices for the entire family. Thus, with the help of various brands focused on serving separate target audience Gap has been able to penetrate different market segments. While the company's value brands help Gap to effectively cater to the increasing base of price sensitive

customers, its upscale brands hold great potential as the US and European economies improve and customer spending increases.

High margins compared to competitors

Over the past few years, Gap has been able to maintain high profit margins compared with its competitors. In FY2013, the company's operating margin was 12.4%. In comparison, the operating margin of ANN, Gap's key competitor, was 7% for the financial year ending January 2013, and the operating margin of another competitor American Eagle Outfitters was 11.4% for the financial year ending January 2013. The company's net profit margin was 7.3% for FY2013, higher compared to the net profit margin of ANN (4.3%) and American Eagle Outfitters (6.7%). High profitability provides a cushion to sustain low revenue growth. Additionally, higher profits compared to competitors would enable Gap to weather price competition effectively.

Weaknesses

Dependence on outside merchandise vendors for supply of products

Gap is completely dependent on outside merchandise vendors for sourcing its products. The company does not own any factories. Gap procures private label and non-private label merchandise from more than 1,000 vendors. Only 2% of the company's merchandise purchased in FY2013 was produced in the US. The remaining 98% of the merchandise was produced in various other countries, with China being one of the largest suppliers. Complete dependence on outside vendors for merchandise procurement reduces Gap's control on the quality of the finished products. In the past, Gap has recalled some of its merchandise procured from China as well as Indonesia.

In April 2013, the company recalled various babyGap footed one-piece sleepers and a sleep gown as these products did not meet the flammability requirements for children's sleepwear under Canadian law. The affected products were sold from November 2012 to February 2013. In July 2012, Old Navy recalled about 34,000 toddler girl aqua socks from the US and about 3,800 from Canada due to slip and fall hazard. In 2010, the company recalled 6,500 swimsuits from the US market and about 480 from the Canadian market. The swimsuits posed a strangulation hazard to children.

Thus, complete dependence on outside vendors for merchandise procurement makes Gap vulnerable to issues such as lack of quality which, in turn, could adversely affect its brand image as well as demand for its products.

Opportunities

Growing e-commerce market

The global e-commerce market is growing at a fast pace and the trend is expected to continue. According to the US Census Bureau, online retail sales (adjusted for seasonal variation) in the US increased from $142.6 billion in 2009 to $224.4 billion in 2012, representing a compound annual growth rate (CAGR) of 16%. E-commerce sales increased 16.3% in 2012 over the previous year.

Total retail sales, on the other hand, grew by only 5.1% in 2012. E-commerce sales accounted for 5.2% of total retail sales in 2012, compared to 4% in 2009. E-commerce sales for the second quarter of 2013 totaled approximately $64.8 billion, an increase of 18.4% from the second quarter of 2012.

A similar trend is noticed in the European market. According to industry estimates, the online retail sales in Europe will reach $255 billion by 2017, a 70% increase over 2012. The Asian market is also expected to witness strong growth in online retail sales in the next few years, driven by strong growth rates in China and India. The Chinese online market, in particular, registered a significant growth rate of over 70% during 2009–12, surpassing $200 billion according to industry sources.

Internet retail has several counter recessionary characteristics like low operational costs which can be passed on to the customers. Additionally, customers prefer online shopping as it is convenient and easy. Apart from retail stores, Gap also sells merchandise through e-commerce sales channel for each of its web-based brands: gap.com, oldnavy.gap.com, bananarepublic.gap.com, piperlime.gap.com, athleta.gap.com and intermixonline.com. Hence, increased online spending will yield high returns on investments. Established presence in this channel will drive Gap's addressable market and top line growth.

Growing apparel industry

The apparel industry has witnessed sluggish growth in the last few years as the demand declined due to several factors, including the economic slowdown in the developed markets, and the fluctuations in the raw material prices which led to an increase in the prices. With the economic condition in developed markets improving leading to an increase in consumer spending, and the strong demand from markets such as India and China due to the increase in disposable income levels, the global apparel market is expected to perform well in the next few years. According to industry estimates, the total apparel sales in the US increased by 3.6% in the first half of 2013, compared to the same time period last year. The men's apparel sales registered the highest increase of 6%, followed by women's apparel at 2.1%. Although the unit sales for men's apparel grew at a lower rate compared to that of the women's apparel, the increase in average selling price led to the higher growth rate for sales of men's apparel. Furthermore, an increase in spending by women in upscale stores was noticed, as more emphasis was laid on individual preferences. Also, industry analysts cited strong growth in the online purchases of apparel in 2012.The growing online spending is also expected to contribute to the growth of the apparel market across geographies. Positive outlook for the apparel industry is expected to augur well for the company's revenue growth in the short to medium term.

Expansion into the growing luxury retail market
In order to penetrate into the higher-end apparel market with an established brand, Gap acquired INTERMIX Holdco, a multi-brand specialty retailer of luxury and contemporary women's apparel and accessories, in December 2012. INTERMIX operates 32 boutiques across North America, along with an e-commerce site, offering a mix of luxury brands from design houses such as Yigal Azrouel, Yves Saint Laurent, Brian Atwood, and Jimmy Choo. This acquisition extends Gap's portfolio of brands, building upon the company's acquisition of Athleta in 2008 and the multi-brand, premium product offering at Piperlime. The luxury market has been registering strong growth globally, driven by the demand from emerging markets across Latin America, Asia Pacific and Africa. The strengthening consumer confidence in some developed markets is also expected to contribute to the growth in the future. According to industry estimates, the global luxury goods sales are estimated to surpass $315 billion in 2013, representing a 3% increase over last year. The addition of Intermix brand to its offering will help Gap to compete better in the growing global luxury retail market.

Expanding presence in Asian markets
Gap has been expanding its presence in Asian markets in the recent years. Gap entered the Chinese retail market in late 2010 with four stores in Beijing and Shanghai, and has since grown to include both Gap specialty and Gap Outlet stores with more than 40 locations across the country by the end of FY2013. The Chinese retail market is expected to grow at a fast pace. Key factors that contribute to the retail market expansion in China include positive economic trends, rising population and increasing wealth of individuals. The company continues to expand its presence in this growth market by opening more stores in 2013. In August 2013, Gap announced plans to introduce the Old Navy brand in China with the opening of its first store in Shanghai and an e-commerce site launching in the first half of 2014. The company announced the opening of its first franchise-operated Old Navy stores in the Philippines in the beginning of 2014, in September 2013.The company plans to expand Gap brand's presence in the Asia region with the opening of its first store in Taipei, Taiwan in the first half of 2014. It also plans to launch a dedicated e-commerce site for the market. Gap has been focusing on strengthening the presence of the Old Navy brand in Japan, one of its key markets for the Gap and Banana Republic brands. In March 2013, Gap announced plans to open nearly 20 more Old Navy stores in Japan in 2013. The brand will launch stores in key areas of Japan, including Nagoya, Kobe,

Osaka and Yokohama. The positive trends and robust growth rates in Asian markets would lend pace to Gap's revenue growth. This, in turn, will help Gap to increase its customer base and thereby improve its top line growth.

Threats

Increasing labor costs

Labor costs have risen in the US and Europe in recent years. Tight labor markets increased overtime, government mandated increases in minimum wages and a higher proportion of full-time employees are resulting in an increase in labor costs. The federal minimum wage rate in the US, which remained at $5.15 per hour since 1998, increased to $5.85 per hour in 2008. It further increased to $6.55 per hour in 2009 and to $7.25 per hour in 2010. Furthermore, many states and municipalities in the country have minimum wage rate even higher than $7.25 per hour due to higher cost of living. The minimum wage rate has increased in the states of Arizona (from $7.65 in 2012 to $7.80 in 2013), Colorado (from $7.64 in 2012 to $7.78 in 2013), Florida (from $7.67 in 2012 to $7.79 in 2013), Ohio (from $7.70 in 2012 to $7.85 in 2013), Oregon (from $8.80 in 2012 to $8.95 in 2013) and Washington (from $9.04 in 2012 to $9.19 in 2013) in the recent past. Similarly, hourly labor costs in the Euro area increased by 0.9% in the year up to the second quarter of 2013. In the EU, the annual rise was 0.9% up to the second quarter of 2013. Moreover, the minimum wages in China have been increasing indicating that the labor costs for Gap could witness an increase as the company is increasing its presence in the country. Minimum wages were adjusted in 23 regions across China in 2012, including Beijing, Sichuan, Jiangxi, Shaanxi, Shenzhen, Shangdong, Shanghai, Tianjin, Guangxi, Ningxia, Gansu, Shanxi, Yunnan, Chongqing, Jiangsu, Xinjiang, Fujian, Hainan, Qinghai, Hunan, Hebei, Inner Mongolia and Heilongjiang. Furthermore, Zhejiang, Beijing, Henan and Shaanxi increased their minimum wage levels effective

January 1, 2013. Beijing has the highest minimum wage rate in China at CNY15.2 per hour ($2.3 per hour), followed by Xinjiang and Shenzhen at CNY13.4 per hour ($2.1 per hour) and CNY13.3 per hour ($2.1 per hour), respectively. China plans to increase the nationwide minimum monthly wage by 13% annually until 2015. Increasing labor costs could increase the company's operating cost and adversely affect its margins.

Growing market for counterfeit products

Existence of counterfeit goods and accessories has proliferated in the recent times. Some of the major factors that led to an increased trade in counterfeit products include growing internet usage, extension of international supply chains and more recently, the global economic downturn that led customers to look for low cost alternatives. Designer sunglasses, footwear, watches, handbags and branded T-shirts are some of the most counterfeited goods present in the market. Local flea markets have also become popular destinations to buy counterfeit products as they offer recession strapped consumers, counterfeit products of popular brands at discounted prices. According to the Intellectual Property Rights (IPR) Seizure Statistics by Customs and Border Protection (CBP) Office of International Trade, the number of IPR seizures reached 22,848 in 2012. The counterfeit trade in handbags / wallets, watches/jewelry, wearing apparel/accessories and footwear accounted for 40%, 15%, 11% and 8%, respectively, of the total manufacturer's suggested retail price of the seizures in 2012. Furthermore, according to the European Commission, the number of detention cases registered by customs totaled 90,473 in 2012. Of these, the number of detention cases registered under clothing (ready- to-wear), perfumes and cosmetics, watches, and jewelry and other accessories categories were 15,007, 2,731, 7,376, and 1,291, respectively.

Most recently, in June 2013, the US Immigration and Customs Enforcement's, Homeland Security Investigations and several law enforcement agencies in Europe, coordinated by the European Police Office (Europol), announced the seizure of 328 Internet domains selling counterfeit merchandise on-line. Rampant existence of counterfeit products poses a major problem to manufacturers as well as retailers of branded goods. Widespread counterfeiting reduces the exclusivity of the company's products. Counterfeits not only deprive Gap of revenues, but also dilute its exclusivity and brand image.

Market Share Data Graph

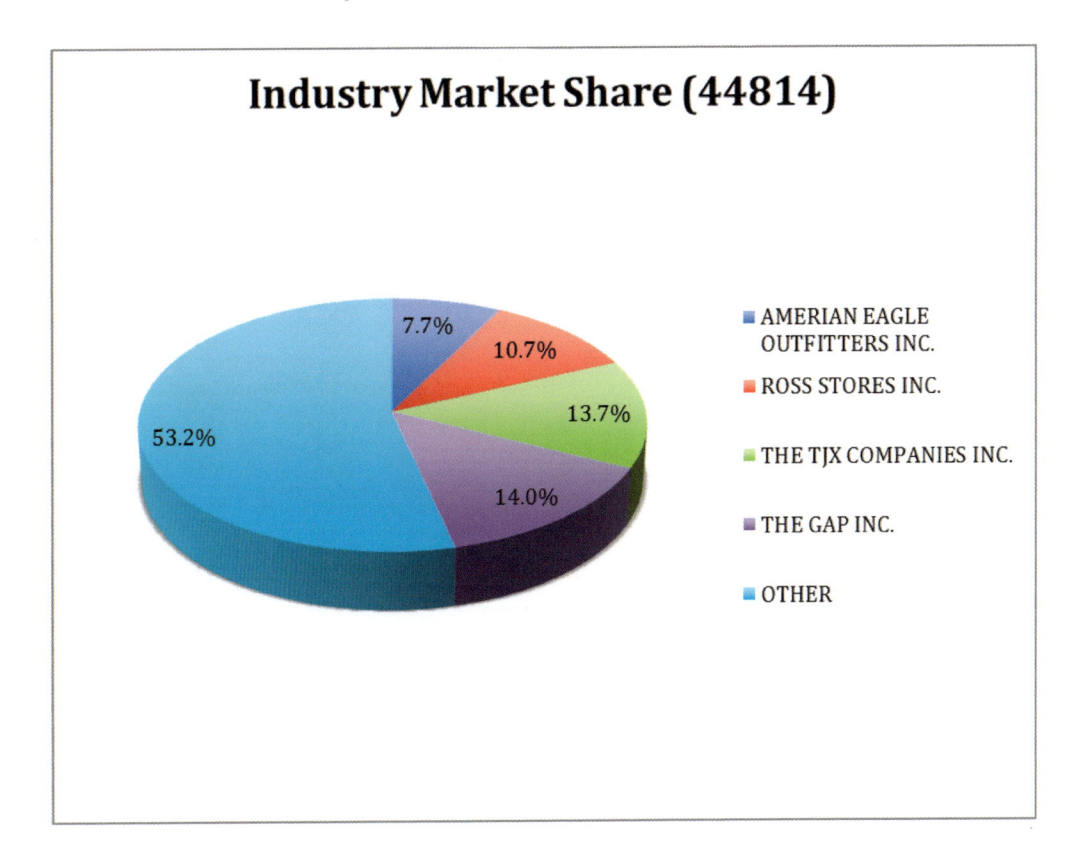

Industry Market Share (44814)

- AMERIAN EAGLE OUTFITTERS INC. — 7.7%
- ROSS STORES INC. — 10.7%
- THE TJX COMPANIES INC. — 13.7%
- THE GAP INC. — 14.0%
- OTHER — 53.2%

In 2013, The Gap Inc. is the industry market share leader with 14 percent of the total market share, emphasizing its superiority with total revenue of 12.8 billion dollars. The total amount of revenue for the industry is 97.8 billion dollars for 2013.

The TJX Companies Inc. (TJX)
With 12.56 billion total revenue in 2013, The TJX Companies, Inc. followed closely behind Gap Inc. The company operates as an off-price retailer of apparel and home fashions that operates in the United States through its TJ Maxx, Marshalls and AJ Wright stores TJ X traces its origins back to 1956 with the opening of Zayre in Massachusetts. The family apparel and accessories retailer sells merchandise at about 800 locations. TJX also has international operations with HomeSense and Winners Apparel stores in Canada, and TK Maxx stores in the United Kingdom and Ireland. The retailer targets middle-income families and fashion-conscious women between the ages of 25 and 54.

TJX Business Units:
- Marmaxx (U.S.)
  T.J. Maxx- offers family apparel, home fashions, merchandise and offers a larger assortment of fine jewelry and accessories than Marshalls.

Marshalls- offers family apparel, home fashions, merchandise, and offers a full line of footwear and broader men's and junior's offerings.
- HomeGoods (U.S.)
  Is an off- price retail chain offering a wide range of home furnishings
- A.J. Wright (U.S.)
  Offers off-price home furnishings and family apparel that targets lower middle-income consumers. As a result of a consolidation, in 2012 A.J. Wright was either converted to T.J. Maxx, Marshalls, HomeGoods, or closed down
- TJX Canada
- TJX Europe

Ross Stores Inc. (ROST)

With 10.7% market share, Ross Stores has become an industry leader totaling 9.72 billion dollars of revenue in 2013. Similar to TJX, it operates a chain of discount apparel retail stores for men, women and children, and the company specifically targets value-conscious consumers between the ages of 25 and 54. The company offers brand name and designer merchandise at low prices and reduces production costs by offering minimal levels of customer service and a no-frills shopping environment in its estimated 900 US stores. Ross Stores, Inc. was founded in 1957 and is headquartered in Pleasanton, California. Ross Stores began in 1982 with six stores in the San Francisco Bay area. After the company went public in 1985, it continuously expanded throughout the United States.

Business Units under ROST (U.S.):
- Ross Dress for Less
  Off-price family apparel store.
- dd's Discounts
  Similar to Ross Dress for Less but offers deeper discounts (dd abbreviation)

American Eagle Outfitters Inc. (AEO)

Trailing behind the market leaders with a 7.7% market share and total revenue of 7.57 billion in 2013, American Eagle had been able to maintain a substantial portion of the U.S. industry. American Eagle is a leading clothing retailer that sells clothing, accessories and personal care products through its subsidiaries, AEO, Inc.. The company designs, markets and sells its own brand of clothing under American Eagle Outfitters, aerie by American Eagle and MARTIN + OSA brand names. American Eagle Outfitters, Inc. was founded in 1977 and is headquartered in Pittsburgh, Pennsylvania. The company primarily operates in the US. The company's retail stores offer denims, sweaters, fleece, outerwear, graphic T-shirts, footwear, and accessories.

The company primarily targets 15 to 25-year old men and women under the American Eagle Outfitters brand name. As of February 2, 2013, it operated 893 American Eagle Outfitters stores and 151 aerie stand-alone stores, as well as 49 franchised stores in 13 countries. The company also extends its business through e-commerce Websites.

Business Units under AEO:
- American Eagle Outfitters
  Offers Junior Men's and Women's apparel
- aeire
  Lingerie retail chain
- Martin + Osa
  Offers apparel targeted towards men and women aged 28-40 years old
- 77kids
  offers children's apparel for ages 2-10 years old

Focal Points for Action
Risk Factors
- Global economic conditions and the impact on consumer spending patterns could adversely impact our results of operations.
- Our business is highly competitive.
- We must successfully gauge apparel trends and changing consumer preferences to succeed.
- Our business, including our costs and supply chain, is subject to risks associated with global sourcing and manufacturing.
- Our efforts to expand internationally may not be successful.
- Our franchise business is subject to certain risks not directly within our control and could impair the value of our brands.
- The market for prime real estate is competitive.
- We experience fluctuations in our comparable sales and margins.
- Changes in our credit profile or deterioration in market conditions may limit our access to the capital markets and adversely impact our financial results or our business initiatives.
- Trade matters may disrupt our supply chain.
- Updates or changes to our IT systems may disrupt operations.
- Our IT services agreement with IBM could cause disruptions in our operations and have an adverse effect on our financial results.
- We are subject to cyber security risks and may incur increasing costs in an effort to minimize those risks.
- Our results could be adversely affected by natural disasters, public health crises, political crises, or other catastrophic events.
- Failure of our vendors to adhere to our code of vendor conduct could harm our business.
- Changes in the regulatory or administrative landscape could adversely affect our financial condition and results of operations.

Concentrating on a company's threats and weaknesses are crucial in protecting and achieving a strategic position in a global environment. Organizations can significantly improve company performance and deliver shareholder value in these areas. Focusing on threats and weaknesses, we are able to correct and move forward to our strategic goals.

Short Range

- Declining sales growth in existing markets
- Return on assets declining
- Highly competitive industry
- Consumer taste constantly changing
- Growing market for counterfeit products

Long Range

- Slow economic recovery
- Dependence on U.S. sales due to concentration of sales when compared to foreign markets
- Increased product costs effect profitability
- Uncertainty for costs of raw material
- Increasing labor costs
- Dependence on outside merchandise vendors to supply products

Develop Alternatives

Industry Type & Characteristics

Current industry segments, show that Generation X (those born between 1960 and 1980) accounts for the largest share of revenue for the Family Clothing Store industry. This segments includes consumers that are characterized as being price conscious who make purchases for themselves, children, and significant others. This is mostly due because this generation would currently carry the responsibility of having a family during this stage in their life. Nonetheless, Gap Inc. should turn its focus to the next generation, which is coming of age, Generation Y (those born between 1980-2000). These consumers are characterized by being more brand-conscious and prefer to shop at specialty stores that carry more visible brands. With this in mind, Gap Inc. should focus more on fashion over functionality on its products while reestablishing their brands. In this sense, Gap Inc. would pursue a product development strategy. Their Gap stores had been able to provide apparel basics that enable consumers to create their own style. Gap may be able to reinforce this strategy while also accommodating to some fashion trends.

Boston Consulting Group Matrix

In order to explain where GAP Inc. is position competitively we've provided the following data dated back in 2009.

The global market industry growth was 2%, in 2009. TJX held the position of global leader in this industry with 1.8% of the market share. The Gap, Inc. captured 1.4% of the market share and 78% of the relative market share. Unfortunately, The Gap, Inc. has become a sleeping dog globally, due to the lower relative market share, slow growth of the industry and the significant fragmentation of the industry. However, this company's executives should not put plans in motion to divest its stake in the global market, because the International Division of the Gap, Inc. is a formidable global competitor. It is ranked as the third out of four global market leaders. Domestically, The Gap, Inc. was the leader in 2009, with a relative market share of 12.5% and a relative market share of 104%. The closest competitor to this Cash Cow was TJX, with 12% of the market share.

The matrix below is an illustration of the position of the Gap, Inc. globally (arrow by dog) and domestically (arrow by cash cow).

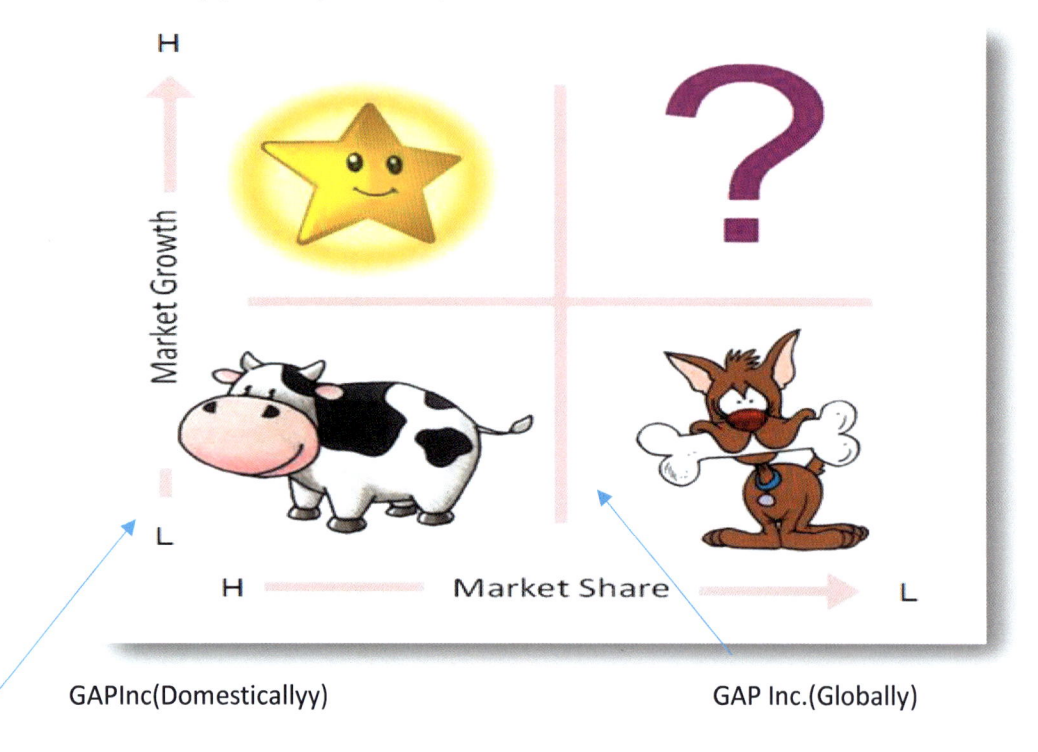

GAPInc(Domesticallyy) GAP Inc.(Globally)

Competitive Position

Competitive Strategy Options-Overall low cost leader-ship/differentiation/focus
Gap Inc. currently fits a Leadership competitive position. The company has been able to attract various consumer segments through its various company specialty store brands. Each company brand carries its own brand name products unlike Gap Inc.'s competitors such as T.J. Maxx and Ross Stores Inc. Because each of Gap Inc.'s brand names is focused on attracting different market segments, Gap Inc. may choose to expand its market share further by expanding its brands. In pursuing this strategy, Gap Inc. can select to engage in horizontal integration, by purchasing other brand name companies to expand its market. The strategy will help Gap Inc. remain a leader in the industry.

Old Navy- This brand offers value-priced apparel, shoes, and accessories and would be most attractive to the Generation X consumer Segment.

The Gap (store brand) - This brand offers an extensive range of apparel at moderate price points. The product range extends from newborn through adult apparel, as well as maternity apparel. The brand includes GapKids, babyGap, and GapBody that offers sports and active apparel.

Banana Republic- This brand offers quality-valued apparel, handbags, shoes, jewelry, and eyewear at higher price points than the Gap brand.

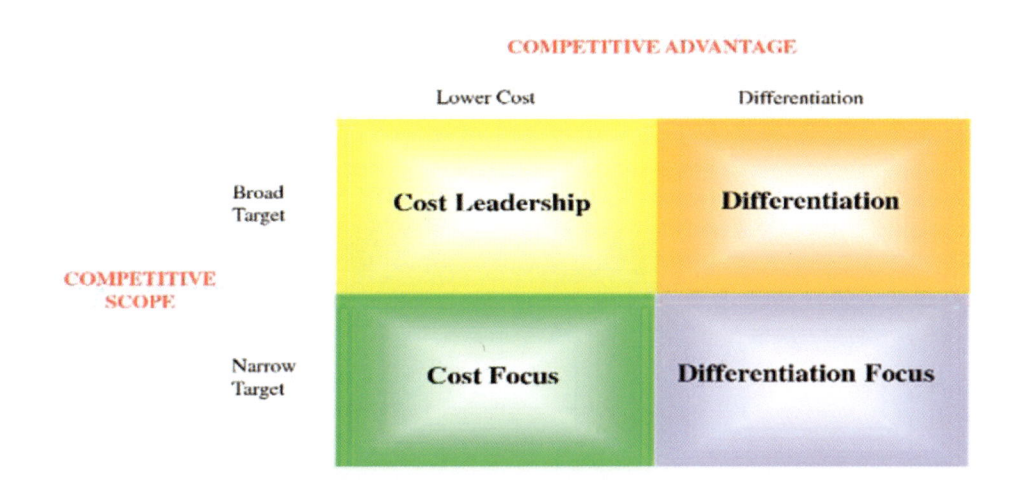

COMPETITIVE ADVANTAGE

	Lower Cost	Differentiation
Broad Target	Cost Leadership	Differentiation
Narrow Target	Cost Focus	Differentiation Focus

COMPETITIVE SCOPE

The above picture illustrates where Gap Inc. falls within Porters Generic Strategies. Though Gap Inc., operates moderate-high end stores such as Banana Republic and Gap, their Old Navy brand carries a strategy to provide low cost products to all types of consumers.

Competitive Strategy Option

As buying power increases for the brand and fashion conscious Generation Y consumer segment, Gap Inc. may choose to pursue a Broad Differentiation Strategy. This strategy will assist GAP Inc. by allowing the company to demand a premium price and increase unit sales by attracting a wider variety of market segments. This strategy may be linked with product development and horizontal integration, allowing the company to establish a broad set of differentiated brand products. In doing so, Gap Inc., will be able to empower brand loyalty which is a characteristic of the emerging Generation Y consumers.

GAP INC. RUMELT'S CRITERIA

STRATEGY	CONSISTENCY	CONSONANCE	FEASIBILITY	ADVANTAGE
Market Penetration				
Billboard Promotions & E-Commerce	4	4	4	4
Tele-Marketing	3	3	3	3
Aggressive Sales Initiatives	5	5	5	4
Market Development				
Develop into Europe	4	4	4	4
Develop into Asia	4	3	4	4
Product Development				
Plus+ Size Attire	5	4	5	4
Outdoor Apparel	4	3	3	4
Shoes	5	5	5	4
Diversification				
Acquire Cache or Charlotte Russe (Women's Apparel)	4	4	3	4
Horizontal Integration				
Acquire ZARA	4	4	2	2
Acquire GILLY HICK	4	4	2	3
Acquire H & M	4	4	3	3
Backward Vertical Integration				
Acquire Xiamen NAJ Commercial Business (clothing manufacturer)	4	4	4	4
Forward Vertical Integration				
Growth of franchisee chains	3	2	4	4
Acquire & Retain retail chains	4	3	4	2

Decision and Recommendations

Corporate

Deliver strong gross margins.

- Increase sales by 7% over the next three years.
- Decrease operating expenses by 2% over the next three years.
- Using effective pricing strategies
- Diverse market penetration
- Optimizing store performance

Manage expenses in a disciplined manner

- Decrease the cost of merchandise by acquiring in the international growth market a local cotton producer factory. This will reduce transportation cost.
- Minimizing inventory holdings will reduce overhead costs.

Return excess cash to shareholders

- Distribute $1.3 billion through dividends and share repurchases.

Business

- Continue to expand internationally.
    - Open additional Gap stores and Old Navy in China.
    - Expand to the Asia region beginning with Taiwan
    - Expand the global outlet presence
    - Continue to grow global growth with digital innovation.
    - Open the first franchise operated Old Navy store
    - Open the first Gap store in Paraguay.
    - Open the first two gap store in Hungary.
    - Open the first Banana Republic in Mexico

Functional

Manage inventory effectively

- To maintain inventory ratios favorable, inventory should be managed effectively. Excessive inventory may cause excessive markdowns creating lower than planned margins. Develop a more effective inventory control system with the Supply Chain Department to be able to react more effective and efficient with customer demands.

Retain Key Personnel

- Motivate talented employees with challenging projects.
- Offer competitive compensation benefits
- Implement incentive programs to motivate employees.
- Offer flexibility within the work schedule such as working from home and summer hours.

Attract customers both in stores and online

- Offer the same sales and coupons in the stores and online.
- Offer affordable shipping rates to encourage online shopping.
- Develop an incentive program for customers both in stores and online to complete a customer feedback survey

Implementation

Goal: Invest in information technologies to track merchandise

Participants: IT, Executives, Management

Steps:

- Increase access to color and size trends
- Lean levels of inventory
- Stock replenishment
- Mark-down determination
- Improve inventory mix

Goal: Acquire more brands with room for expansion

Participants: Marketing, R & D, Executives, Management, Board of Directors

Steps:

- Gap and Old Navy are considered Old Brands
- Create new fashions
- Invest in up-and-coming retailers
- Acquire Intermix (a multi-brand specialty retailer)

Goal: Global expansion through franchising

Participants: Executives, Board of Director, Management

Steps:

- Establish planning committee
- Research geographic areas for franchise expansion
- Determine short and long-term goals
- Determine financial cost
- Establish franchise committee
- Communicate with shareholders, stakeholders, suppliers, retailers, employees and consumers
- Formalize franchise process with 8 Latin American countries

Goal: Reduce number of suppliers

Participants: Management, Executives,

- Currently utilizing 1,000 vendors
- 98% of merchandise purchased outside of the U.S.
- Implement fire safety standards for suppliers
- Create efficiency
- Acquire an international manufacturer to reduce currency exchange rates
- Increase control over quality of product

Goal: Increase Social Media presence

Participants: Marketing, Sales, IT Department, Finance

Steps:

- Identify target market for high traffic social media sites
- Establish steps to increase brand awareness on social media sites
- Determine financial costs
- Develop plans to consistently post and advertise
- Engage employees with straightforward Social Media Policy
- Offer instant deals or coupons to social media consumers

Bibliography

Gap Incorporated (The)
Copyright 2013 W/D Partners Worldscope February 1, 2014

Ross Stores Incorporated
Copyright 2013 W/D Partners Worldscope February 1, 20014

TJX Companies, Inc.
Copyright 2013 W/D Partners Worldscope February 1, 2014

American Eagle Outfitters
Copyright 2013 W/D Partners Worldscope February 1, 2014

Lovero, Eveann, Strategic Management Syllabus. Lewis University 2014

The Gap, Inc. 2012 Annual Report
http://investors.gapinc.com/phoenix.zhtml?c=11302&p=irol-reports Annual

The GPS, The Gap, Inc.
http://finance.yahoo.com

Thompson, Arthur A., Peteraf, Margaret A., Gamble, John E, Strickland III, A.J., eds. 18th .Crafting and Executing Strategy. New York. McGraw-Hill/Irwin a division of The McGraw-Hill Companies, Inc. 2012

Printed in Great Britain
by Amazon